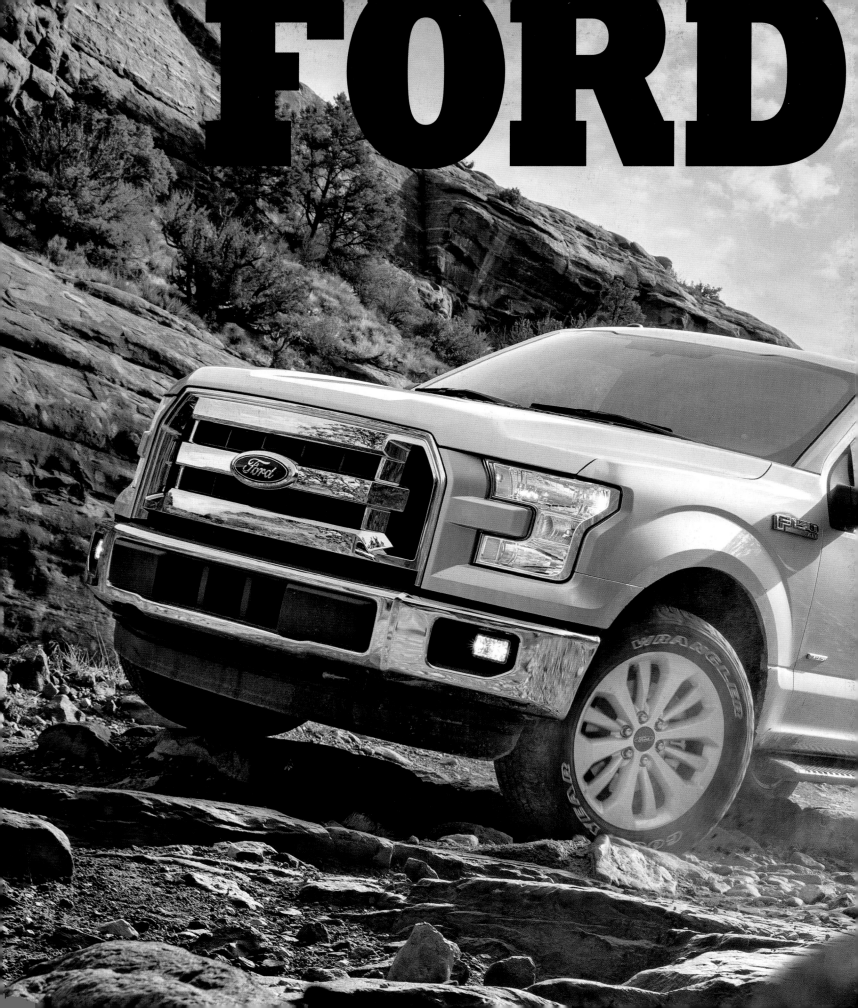

TOUGH

100 Years
OF FORD TRUCKS

PATRICK FOSTER

motorbooks

Brimming with creative inspiration, how-to projects, and useful information to enrich your everyday life, Quarto Knows is a favourite destination for those pursuing their interests and passions. Visit our site and dig deeper with our books into your area of interest: Quarto Creates, Quarto Cooks, Quarto Homes, Quarto Lives, Quarto Drives, Quarto Explores, Quarto Gifts, or Quarto Kids.

To the memory of my parents, Wilfred and Liane Foster.

First published in 2017 by Motorbooks, an imprint of The Quarto Group, 401 Second Avenue North, Suite 310, Minneapolis, MN 55401 USA.
T: (612) 344-8100 F: (612) 344-8692   QuartoKnows.com

Motorbooks titles are also available at discount for retail, wholesale, promotional, and bulk purchase. For details, contact the Special Sales Manager by email at specialsales@quarto.com or by mail at The Quarto Group, Attn: Special Sales Manager, 401 Second Avenue North, Suite 310, Minneapolis, MN 55401 USA.

10 9 8 7 6 5 4 3 2 1

ISBN: 978-0-7603-5217-5

Library of Congress control number: 2016963834

Acquiring Editor: Darwin Holmstrom
Project Manager: Caitlin Fultz
Art Director: James Kegley
Layout: Diana Boger

On the front cover: 1965 advertisement for the Twin I-Beam.
On the back cover: 2017 F-150 SuperCab with the Special Edition package.
On the title page: 2016 Ford F-150.
On the endpapers: FRONT: 1953 Ford F-100 pickup. BACK: 2017 Ford F-150 Raptor.

Printed in China

CONTENTS

INTRODUCTION

IF AT FIRST YOU DON'T SUCCEED

If an absolute refusal to give up on a dream counts for anything, Henry Ford was bound to succeed. The former superintendent of the Edison Illuminating Company in Detroit was a natural mechanic, a self-taught engineer, and a visionary thinker. After designing and building a self-propelled gasoline-engine buggy for his own use in 1896, Ford became determined to be an automobile manufacturer. Three years later, in August 1899, Ford and a group of local investors organized the Detroit Automobile Company, which produced its first vehicle, a commercial delivery wagon, in January 1900. During the ensuing months the infant firm built a number of automobiles but by year-end was out of business, many of its backers blaming Ford. He had the skills to design a car but apparently lacked the ability to run a profitable business. Rather than focus on building cars in quantity, he'd spent too much time experimenting with new ideas and developing additional car models.

Here's a Model T roadster fitted with what appears to be a home-built wooden pickup box. Apparently this unit was built by a dealer for use as a service car for the dealership's service department. Although Ford says this photo is a 1915 model, other sources have claimed it is a 1912 model.

Undeterred by this setback, Henry Ford decided to continue to experiment with new engineering notions and even built racing cars to try out some of his ideas, quickly growing a reputation as a talented automotive engineer and daring race car driver. Then in November 1901 he got a second chance when his new enterprise, the Henry Ford Company, was incorporated with a new group of investors. Although the company got off to a good start, it wasn't long before Ford became disenchanted with his backers; within three months of its founding, Ford resigned from the firm, taking his name with him. Truth be told, many of Ford's backers had become disenchanted with him as well. The investors wanted to produce larger, more expensive cars that would yield big profits, while Ford wanted to produce small, inexpensive cars that could sell in large volumes. He spoke of something that seemed impossible: a car for the masses, affordable for the average man. Sometime after he left the fold, the Henry Ford Company was reorganized as the Cadillac Automobile Company. It went on, of course, to become one of the most successful of the early carmakers.

Henry's third try, the one that would prove successful, began on June 16, 1903, when the Ford Motor Company was established, with Henry Ford serving as vice president and chief engineer and holding 25.5 percent of its stock, which was given to him in exchange for his designs and expertise.

Ford was joined in his efforts by a team of men who each held skills needed to ensure the new enterprise would be successful. Electrician and mechanic Edward "Spider" Huff was an old friend who helped build many of the prototype components used in the cars, while Childe Harold Wills, a talented draftsman, was the man who expertly put Henry's ideas to paper so they could be produced in quantity. Detroit coal merchant Alex Malcomson put up money to get the company started, while his chief clerk, James Couzens, kept an eye on the new firm's cashbox and made sure the company was run on a lean and efficient basis. They were joined by a varied group of other investors, all of whom must have felt a little uneasy about Mr. Ford's two previous failures. Couzens, however, had complete faith in Henry's vision and bravely put every dime he had into the new venture. He even convinced his schoolteacher sister to put half of her two hundred dollars in life savings into the company.

One of the investors had a suitable building to rent on Mack Avenue in Detroit for seventy-five dollars per month, so the new firm had a factory in which to build its new car. However, in today's terminology, it would be called an assembly plant rather than a manufacturing plant because rather than manufacture all of the new car's components in-house, which would have called for a much larger investment than the group was capable of securing, the company's leaders decided to farm out production of the most capital-intensive parts and components. Thus, vehicle bodies were produced by the C. R. Wilson Carriage Company, while Ford's engines, transmissions, and axles were produced by a machine shop owned by two hard-drinking hell-raisers, brothers Horace and John Dodge. In time the Dodge boys would become investors in the new firm as well, eventually earning enough money to become automakers themselves. Other suppliers included Lansing's Prudden Wheel Company and the Hartford Rubber Works Company, which provided the wheels and tires for the cars, respectively.

This 1-ton dump truck is a 1918 Model TT and is fitted with an enclosure known as a C-style cab due to the shape of the door opening. Notice, too, the heavier-duty rear wheel and tire.

A PFENNIG FOR YOUR THOUGHTS

The necessary parts and components were purchased or manufactured and automobile assembly soon began, but it was a full month after incorporation before the company sold its first car, to a Chicago dentist named Dr. E. Pfennig. It was a good thing Dr. Pfennig paid for his automobile in full, too, because by that point the total operating cash of the Ford Motor Company had shrunk to a mere $223.65.

The Ford car he purchased was a small two-passenger runabout powered by a two-cylinder gasoline engine developing 8 horsepower. It was hooked up to a 2-speed planetary transmission. Sturdy and well-built, the little Ford was priced at $850. For $100 more a detachable tonneau could be added to the rear to seat two additional passengers.

Thankfully, once the new Ford cars began to sell, the company's bank balance began to rise. Sales were brisk, to put it mildly. By the end of September 1904, the new company had produced more than 1,700 of its Model A Ford runabout cars, making it one of the largest automakers in the country, if not the world. Henry Ford, age forty-one, was on his way to becoming a very rich man.

Chapter 1

EARLY ATTEMPTS

Without a doubt, the Ford Motor Company's focus was on automobiles, not trucks, at least initially. Henry Ford still had a dream of creating a perfect car for the masses, low in cost, easy and economical to run, and absolutely reliable. The Model A, priced at $800 by 1904, was a good start toward his ultimate goal, though Ford was certain he could do better. Other automobile models soon followed, and 1905 marked a minor first attempt at producing a truck. That year the company offered a commercial version of its two-cylinder Model C passenger car by attaching a small delivery-type body to the back end of a new Ford runabout. Only a reported ten units were built, and since they were built on a passenger-car chassis, they didn't really signal a serious attempt to enter the truck market with a dedicated truck chassis.

Here's a 1912 Model T roadster pickup that's been loaded about to its maximum, judging by how low it's riding in the back. Farmers loved these little trucks because they were handy for work around the farm as well as trips to pick up supplies in town.

Get squarely on top of your delivery situation

Light commercial cars are cutting down delivery costs in every industry. How about *your own* delivery problems? Wouldn't you like the facts about light delivery for your business?

BABCOCK BODIES *for* FORD CARS

put within your reach these sturdy, reliable light delivery cars that cost little to get and a great deal less to operate than any other kind of delivery.

Babcock Bodies will save you money for three distinct reasons:

Fit your business. The nine different types furnish every requirement in light transportation. You will save time and money by having the most efficient body for your particular business.

Quality at low cost. Babcock Bodies are built in thousand lots on the unit plan. In this way we can build better bodies for less money, and you get the benefit. Quantity production gives you the utmost quality at the lowest possible cost.

Give maximum service. Babcock Bodies are strong and sturdy for year after year service — well designed — built of specially selected woods — open-hearth steel braces and straps — quality material and thorough workmanship throughout. You get a real dollars-and-cents value in maximum service and freedom from repairs.

Why not talk this over with your Ford Dealer? In the meantime mail us the coupon below for our illustrated booklet.

FORD DEALERS
If you have not received the full details of our sales proposition, write us.

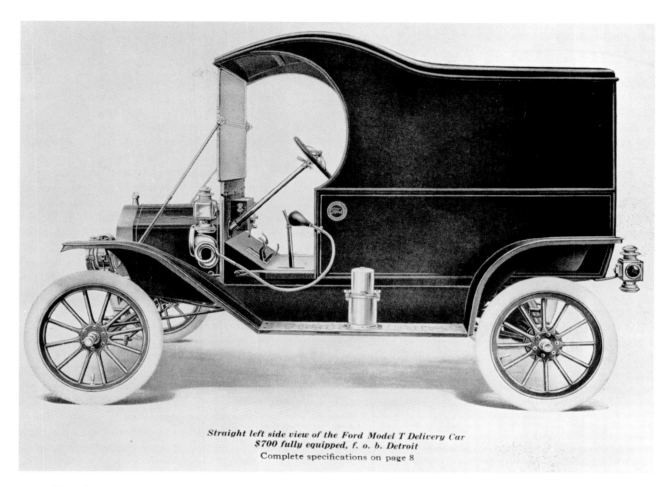

Straight left side view of the Ford Model T Delivery Car
$700 fully equipped, f. o. b. Detroit
Complete specifications on page 8

ABOVE: Although Ford Motor Company didn't officially enter the dedicated truck market until 1917, Ford truck-type vehicles were produced almost from the beginning. The difference was that the early models were built on a passenger-car chassis, whereas starting in 1917 Ford offered true truck chassis designed for heavy-duty jobs. This 1912 Model T delivery car is a perfect example of a car-based commercial vehicle, which were commonly known as "commercial cars."

OPPOSITE: The H. H. Babcock Company of Watertown, New York, manufactured a wide variety of bodies for the Ford Model T chassis. As the ad states, an aftermarket body mounted on a Model T chassis gives the buyer "quality at low cost."

But real attempts would come, that seemed certain. Henry Ford had grown up on a farm, knew and detested farm work, and had inside him a strong desire to make farmers' lives easier. Having a reliable truck to carry farm goods to market would certainly help. But before he could get to the point of focusing his energies on producing a dedicated truck chassis, Henry Ford was going to have to concentrate on growing his company.

In the meantime, the fact that Ford Motor Company didn't produce trucks and commercial vehicles on its own didn't stop others from adapting the Ford vehicle to work usage. Anyone desiring a Ford truck who was handy with woodworking tools could easily hammer together a light delivery body or pickup bed and add it to their existing Ford car, and there's plenty of historical evidence that this was, indeed, done quite often.

In addition, there sprung up numerous small companies that offered pickup truck or delivery body conversions for the Ford car, often for the roadster body style. The introduction of the sturdy, high-volume Model T in late 1908 seems to have brought a greatly increased interest in commercial possibilities for the Ford car. By 1912 the company itself offered a commercial roadster with a removable rumble seat to facilitate hauling. Besides that there was also a $700 delivery car with an enclosed delivery-style

ABOVE: The 1914 Model T screen-side delivery (a.k.a. screen-side express) was in all likelihood created by installing an aftermarket body onto a Ford roadster. This was a common practice back then because it yielded a sturdy lightweight truck at a very low cost.

LEFT: This 1915 Model T is yet another roadster fitted with a slip-on pickup body. Made of steel construction with sturdy flare boards and a double-panel tailgate, this appears to be a high-quality body.

body that provided good protection for the cargo while leaving the driver open to the elements, save for the rounded roof panel and windshield. Reportedly 250 prototype (or pilot line) units of that model were sold to the Bell Telephone Companies in 1910 and 1911 to prove out the design before it became a regular offering to the public for 1912.

FROM AFTERMARKET TO AUTHENTIC

Alas, the delivery car was short-lived and Ford discontinued the model in 1913 due to a lack of interest, along with a desire to simplify product offerings in order to speed up production and drive down costs. As always, however, the aftermarket was ready to provide a range of commercial bodies to fit the Ford chassis. Companies supplying aftermarket commercial bodies for Ford products included McKay Carriage Company of Grove City, Pennsylvania; Smith Form-a-Truck Company of Chicago (which made a complete truck conversion kit); Detroit's own Columbia Body Manufacturing Company; Union Truck Manufacturing Company of New York; Highland Body Manufacturing Company

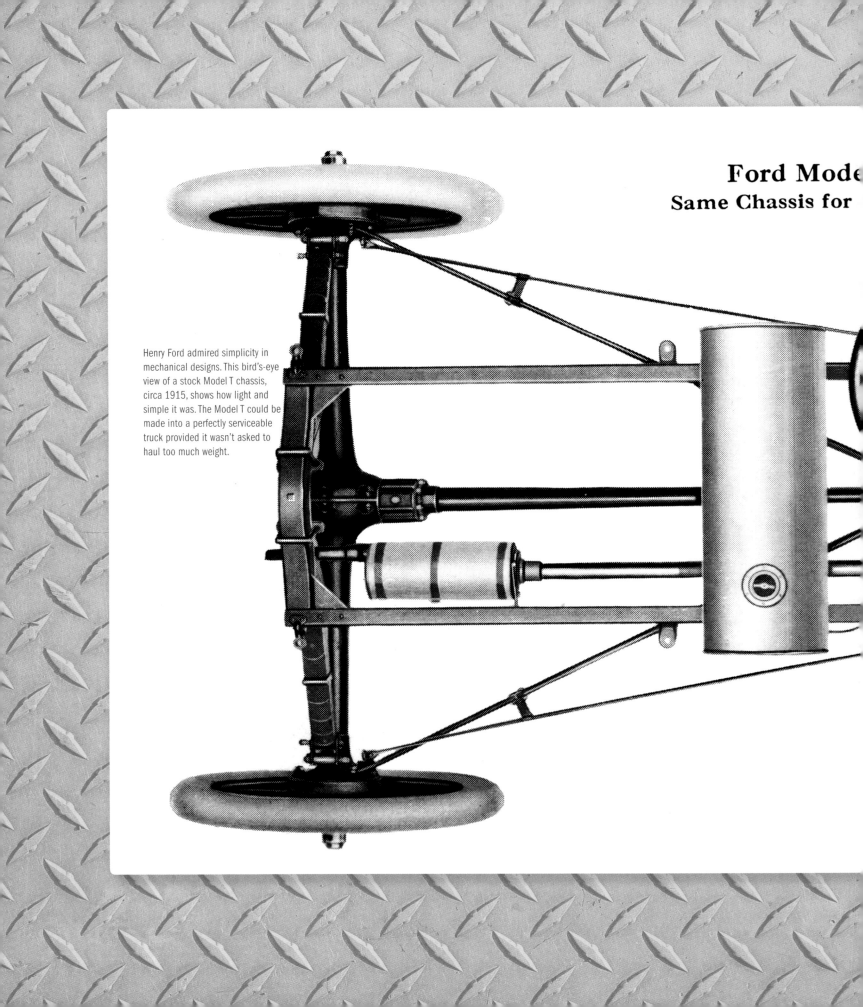

Henry Ford admired simplicity in mechanical designs. This bird's-eye view of a stock Model T chassis, circa 1915, shows how light and simple it was. The Model T could be made into a perfectly serviceable truck provided it wasn't asked to haul too much weight.

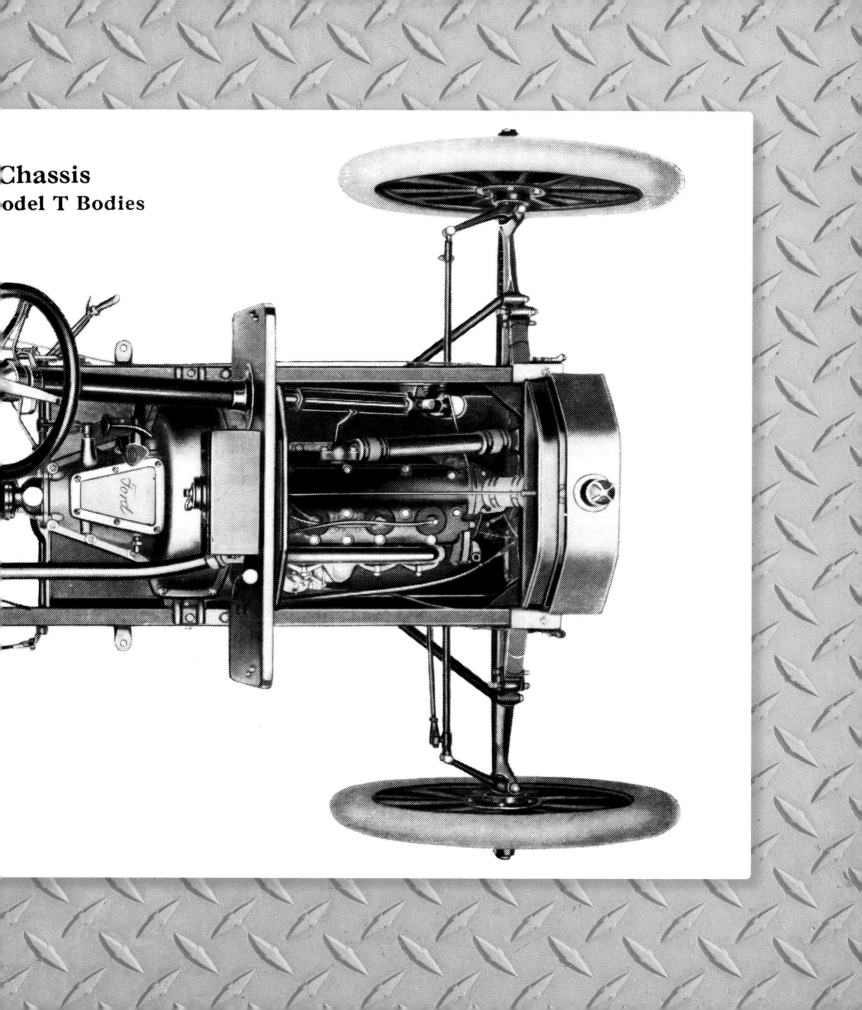

Chassis

odel T Bodies

of Cincinnati; and countless others. There were even companies building medium-duty trailer units to attach to the back of a Ford car, creating an early tractor-trailer type of rig, though we wonder how safe those could have been considering the Ford's simplistic cable-operated two-wheel brakes. One source claims that adding a commercial body to a new Ford voided the manufacturer's warranty, though that hasn't been verified.

Because the Ford Model T was a light car, the maximum cargo capacity of these vehicles was necessarily quite limited, though several enterprising companies included kits to beef up the strength of the Ford's frame, springs, and axles. However, as motor trucks became more common and cargo loads became larger and heavier, it became apparent that adapting a light-duty car chassis to the demands of commercial work was in general not a very good idea. A car was a car, and although for the lightest jobs it could make do as a commercial vehicle, the best solution for most jobs and most businesses was a vehicle built on a dedicated chassis designed for the purpose: a truck, in other words.

By this point Ford Motor Company was ready to commit to such a vehicle. In the period from 1903 to 1916, the once small, underfunded company had grown to become the largest automaker in the country, producing half a million vehicles a year, rolling in cash, and able to undertake projects it hadn't been able to before.

According to published sources, in early 1916 the company sent out a letter to all its dealers prohibiting them from making alterations to new Ford cars in order to accommodate the longer after-market truck bodies, such as the Smith Form-a-Truck conversions. The reasons given might have included that they were not as safe as a factory-engineered truck, nor were they probably as rugged either. However, an announcement that came not long after suggests that Ford was trying to eliminate some of its competition in advance of a project its engineers were working on: an authentic Ford-designed-engineered-and-built truck on a dedicated, commercial chassis of 1-ton capacity.

PREVIOUS PAGES: Henry Ford admired simplicity in mechanical designs. This bird's-eye view of a stock Model T chassis, circa 1915, shows how light and simple it was. The Model T could be made into a perfectly serviceable truck provided it wasn't asked to haul too much weight.

BELOW LEFT: Here's an unusual commercial car: a 1915 Model T coupe equipped with a cooler box for carrying Coca-Cola. One seldom saw coupes converted for commercial use because of the model's higher cost, but in this case it might have been done because of the New York weather. Note the sign on the building "N.Y. Branch—The Coca-Cola Company."

BELOW RIGHT: A Model T could be used as a truck provided it wasn't called upon to carry heavy loads. Operating as a delivery truck for the US Postal Service was a good use of a Model T such as this 1916 model, equipped with a panel delivery body and open cab.

Another Coca-Cola commercial car, this one a 1916 Model T roadster fitted with an unusual box on the rear. This is probably a salesman's car used for bringing samples to customers.

FORD'S FIRST HEAVY-DUTY TRUCK

The new Ford truck boasted a chassis that was specially engineered for tough work. The wheelbase was two feet longer and included a frame that was much more robust than the standard passenger-car frame. The rear suspension was likewise of the heavy-duty type. For added durability, heavy-duty artillery wheels were fitted to the sturdy worm-drive rear axle, along with solid rubber tires. According to the industry trade paper *Automotive News*, just 209 1-ton Ford chassis were produced during the final months of 1916, in an infant American truck market that sold nearly 36,000 trucks that year.* For an automaker of Ford's size and clout, this was an inauspicious beginning for what was destined to become such a huge part of its business. Clearly Ford's new truck enterprise had nowhere to go but up. In fact, in that regard Ford would astound the world!

* All sales numbers in this book are taken from industry trade publications and are based on the calendar year rather than model year.

Chapter 2

FORD ENTERS THE TRUCK MARKET

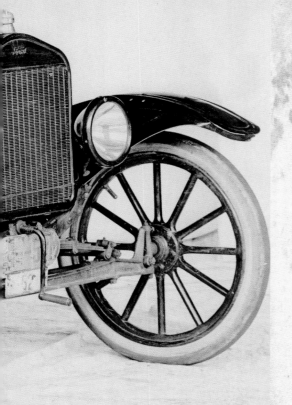

A NEW ERA: THE 1-TON TRUCK CHASSIS

The new Ford 1-ton truck chassis—known internally as the Model TT—was a relative bargain, priced at a mere $600 for the initial 1917 model. While it's true that price was a good deal higher than a Model T chassis at $325, the 1-ton was a heavy-duty workhorse, built for big loads and rough use. It was a real truck chassis, not an overworked car platform, built for the long haul.

Working as a truck driver in the early days of motor trucks was an extremely difficult job. Because of the high cost of enclosed bodies, most trucks in the pre-1920s had cabs that left the driver exposed to the elements. In severe winter areas a canvas enclosure could be added to hold back the elements, as shown on this 1918 model. Even so, many trucks lacked heaters, so although the driver was protected from wind and snow, he was still very cold.

ABOVE: July 27, 1917, was an historic day for the Ford Motor Company because it marked the firm's entry into the truck market with its all-new Model TT 1-ton truck chassis. Prior to this, the only Ford "trucks" had been converted passenger-car chassis.

BELOW: The new Model TT was ruggedly built and an outstanding value—priced at just $600 for the chassis, plus the cost of whatever type of body was installed.

FORD MODEL T ONE TON TRUCK

This is the Model T One Ton Truck just as we deliver to the purchaser, without body. The equipment includes hood for motor, front fenders, stepping boards, two side lights, two head lights, one tail light, horn and set of tools. All Ford cars sold f.o.b. Detroit

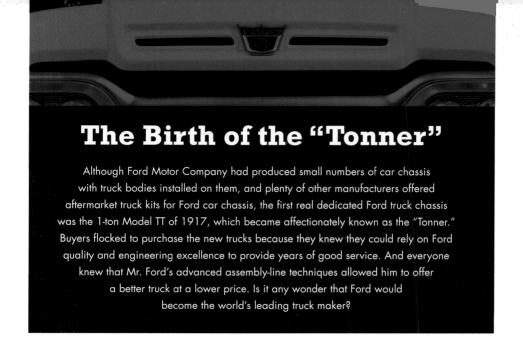

The Birth of the "Tonner"

Although Ford Motor Company had produced small numbers of car chassis
with truck bodies installed on them, and plenty of other manufacturers offered
aftermarket truck kits for Ford car chassis, the first real dedicated Ford truck chassis
was the 1-ton Model TT of 1917, which became affectionately known as the "Tonner."
Buyers flocked to purchase the new trucks because they knew they could rely on Ford
quality and engineering excellence to provide years of good service. And everyone
knew that Mr. Ford's advanced assembly-line techniques allowed him to offer
a better truck at a lower price. Is it any wonder that Ford would
become the world's leading truck maker?

Interestingly, the same model year that Ford launched its new truck chassis, Dodge Brothers also began building complete trucks, starting with a ½-ton screen-side delivery. Horace and John Dodge had been loyal suppliers to Henry Ford, as well as stockholders, but in 1913 they decided to cease being a Ford supplier and go out on their own. Now that they were free to become competitors, their first move had been the introduction of the Dodge Brothers automobile for 1914, along with some car-based light trucks. Now, in 1917, they were becoming a bigger player in the truck market.

Once full-scale production of the dedicated Ford truck chassis got underway in earnest, a veritable flood of body manufacturers introduced special work bodies to be fitted on it. Outside body suppliers included Columbia, which produced bodies for both the 1-ton chassis and the standard Model T chassis; Mifflinburg Body Company in Pennsylvania, one of the more prolific and successful body builders; Field Automatic Steel Body, which produced a popular dump truck body; Martin-Parry Corporation in York; and countless others. In addition, the Prospect Fire Engine Company of Prospect, Ohio, manufactured chemical tank and hose bodies for the Model T runabout. Light and inexpensive, these sturdy little fire trucks proved quite popular with smaller communities that couldn't afford to purchase full-size truck-based fire equipment and were a notable improvement over the horse-drawn fire apparatus that had been the norm. Not surprisingly, light-truck bodies of all types continued to be exceptionally popular, due to the low cost of the Model T platform as well as the ease of body installation.

With the availability of a true Ford heavy-duty truck chassis, the market for heavy-truck bodies was greatly opened up. Some of the 1-ton truck body types that were in production at various companies included coal and oil truck bodies, stake bodies, grain bodies, cattle trucks, moving vans, gravel truck bodies, and more. Mifflinburg alone produced dozens of body types and styles for the Ford chassis. Amazingly, during the 1917 calendar year Ford's US truck sales totaled an extraordinary 41,725 units. Its nearest competitor, the Republic Motor Truck Company, sold about 8,200 vehicles.

At the same time, World War I—or "The Great War" as they called it—was still raging in Europe, and thousands of young men on both sides were dying in hopeless assaults against fortified trench lines. America itself had joined the fight in Europe on April 6, 1917. Because of that conflict there was an enormous demand for military-purpose trucks of all types: troop carriers, cargo trucks, ambulances, artillery tractors, and so forth. Like many other large automotive companies, the Ford Motor Company pitched in to help the Allies in their effort to defeat the forces of Germany and Austria-Hungary. In addition to the heavy-duty truck chassis used to transport men and supplies, the Ford Motor Company in 1917 also produced more than 5,700 military ambulances for the US Army Medical Corps. These were built on the Model T chassis, considered strong enough for such relative light-duty work. In all, Ford produced for the war effort more than 39,000 vehicles in factories located in Britain, the United States, and Canada. In addition, Henry Ford also leased the Henry Ford Hospital in Detroit to the US government for a token fee of one dollar a year. Hundreds of Ford employees volunteered to serve in the armed forces.

Although the war managed to put a crimp in the total production of motor vehicles during 1918, Ford sold over 62,000 trucks that calendar year, a sharp rise from the prior year, making Ford the largest truck company in the world by far. Many of these were produced on the 1-ton TT chassis, some on the standard Model T chassis, and

ABOVE: Yummy! This fleet of pie delivery trucks was owned by Holmes & Son Inc. The company must have been doing pretty well; we count at least seven Model T trucks fitted with panel delivery bodies.

RIGHT: During 1917 Ford Motor Company continued to produce the Model T passenger car and also offered chassis that were converted to truck-type vehicles. One that was vitally needed, due to the ongoing Great War, was this ambulance model. More than 5,700 of these ambulances were produced for the war effort.

The Depot Hack was a body style that used to be quite common. The name was derived from its usage as a taxi (or hack, to use the slang term) that picked up passengers from the train or bus depot. Because they operated like a minibus, these special wooden wagon-type bodies were produced to hold as many passengers as possible. These are the forerunners of the station wagons that became so popular in the 1950s and 1960s. This is a 1925 Model T.

some on strengthened car chassis. Sales were probably boosted by Ford's decision to lower the TT chassis price to $550 during the year.

Thankfully the war ended in November 1918 with the signing of an armistice. Restrictions on civilian vehicle production were lifted, and armed with a great deal of momentum in the marketplace, Ford turned up the dial on truck production.

In addition to its dedicated heavy-truck chassis sales, Ford was growing its light-duty business as well this year. The US Post Office purchased Model T panel trucks for mail delivery, while many hotels purchased wood-bodied station wagons for use as "depot hacks," picking up guests at the train station and transporting them and their luggage to the hotel.

There was a bit of trouble brewing in Dearborn, however. Over the years since the founding of the Ford Motor Company, Henry Ford had become disenchanted with his fellow stockholders, feeling they were restricting his freedom to run the business the way he felt it should be run. During 1919, Ford decided he'd had enough and formed a new firm with the express purpose of buying out the company's remaining minority stockholders. It proved to be a very expensive gambit, but Henry was able to do it and, free of their interference and not beholden to the banks either, began to expand his automaking empire. Work began on a new factory in which all the various aspects of producing an automobile would come together in one continuous motion. Henry Ford envisioned a vast factory complex in which raw materials would enter at one end, they would be processed step by step into necessary parts and components, and finished automobiles would exit at the other end, eliminating all transportation costs of materials and parts as well as lost or wasted motions in vehicle assembly. It would be the largest and most efficient vehicle manufacturing plant in the world.

ABOVE: One of the more popular "trucks" of 1919 wasn't really even a truck; it was a converted Model T roadster with a short pickup bed installed, such as the model shown here. With steel doors and a soft top, this setup actually offered better weather protection than many larger trucks but, of course, couldn't haul much of a load. Still, they were very inexpensive and popular among farmers and small business owners.

RIGHT: For heavier jobs, the right tool was a 1919 Model TT 1-ton truck chassis, as shown here fitted with a Prospect Deluge chemical-and-hose truck body. These were very popular with small towns because of their low price, ease of service, and rugged durability. We wonder if the name "Montpelier Fire Department" painted on the side refers to the small but picturesque capital of Vermont or some other town. Anybody out there know?

Why All the Success?

Why was the Ford Motor Company so successful? For starters, it enjoyed several important advantages over its competitors. The Ford brand name was the best known in the world and well trusted. By this point Henry Ford himself had become a populist among the people, with many folks wanting him to run for president of the United States, so the tide of public sentiment was on his side. To many he seemed to be a man of the people, capable of doing no wrong. People admired him so much they naturally wanted to buy his products. In addition, Ford had the largest and strongest dealer network by far, the best distribution organization, the most efficient factories, and the lowest prices.

Ford Motor Company boasted another great advantage over all other car or truck companies: economies of scale unheard of prior to this time. Because of the incredible sales volume of this popular automaker, truck-body builders nearly always designed new bodies for Ford before doing so for anyone else. In addition, the Ford truck was well engineered, sturdy, and durable. And buyers knew that if anything did go wrong with their Ford truck there were thousands of dealers around the country waiting to help them with parts and repairs. Besides all that, Ford had a broader product range than many of the smaller independent truck brands, and its lineup ranged from the lightest trucks up to heavy-duty 1-ton jobs.

Here we see a 1923 Ford Model TT with a C-side cab and a light express body, useful for lightweight delivery and hauling. In this record year, Ford Motor Company sold over 193,000 trucks, more than six times greater than second-place Chevrolet. Stamina, reliability, and low prices were all factors in Ford's amazing success.

Also popular was this prisoner transporter, used by police departments in most major cities, especially when raiding illicit business establishments. Built on a 1918 Model T chassis, its lightweight construction was necessary due to the engine's low power.

Construction of additions and upgrades continued on to 1928. When it was finally completed, they would call it the River Rouge Plant, and it was an astonishing place to see. All day long, lake freighters pulled up to the docks at the plant's deep-water slips and disgorged their cargos of coal, iron ore, lumber, limestone, and more. Huge blast furnaces and coke ovens worked night and day to transform the raw materials into coke, steel, and iron that then were formed and shaped into the various parts and components that made up the hot-selling Ford cars and trucks.

By any standard, 1919 proved to be an amazing year for Ford trucks with calendar year sales totaling a whopping 120,597 in a truck market that totaled 240,163 units, meaning Ford managed to grab slightly more than half the market. Thirty-five non-Ford brands split up the other half of the market among themselves. The second-place Dodge Brothers Company sold less than 15,000 units.

THE ROARING TWENTIES

The work and business uses for the 1-ton Ford Model TT truck chassis expanded even further during 1920 as bus body manufacturers discovered it to be more than suitable to their needs. Tow trucks were, of course, a natural fit also, as were large moving vans. Companies that transported any sort of heavy freight or cargo soon took a good look at the Ford product and most found it an attractive option. Meanwhile the standard Model

T chassis continued to support fruit wagon bodies, express bodies, and even some prisoner transporters. Ford body suppliers at this point included Calumet Truck Body Corporation, American LaFrance Fire Engine Company, Columbia, Mifflinburg, Atlas, and many others.

Amid all this, 1920 saw a short, sharp recession—history books call it the Depression of 1920–1921, when the US economy took a swift and sudden downturn. Lasting from January 1920 to July 1921, it saw a large drop in gross domestic product coupled with extreme deflation of prices and inventory valuations. Wholesale prices fell a reported 36 percent, the largest drop since the Revolutionary War, and business activities for the most part dried up. Stock market prices also fell sharply while unemployment rose; all in

This photo is identified as a 1920 Ford Model TT panel delivery truck, but it appears to actually be a Model T with a panel truck body installed. The sturdy T chassis could handle light delivery tasks, but for heavier jobs the TT was the preferred choice. Notice this panel truck has an enclosed passenger cab.

RIGHT: Another Model TT truck fitted with a work body is this 1923 stake truck with side racks installed. With a roomy enclosed cab, large windows, side mirror, and cowl lamps, this must have been a pleasure to drive compared to many other trucks on the road. Note the words "Expedited Service" painted on the roof's side panel.

BELOW: A side view of the Jones Transfer truck shows the large cab and wooden stake body. Notice the heavier wheels. Always striving for more sales volume, Ford increased its production capacity this year.

was an extremely scary situation for a while. And though thankfully short-lived, it did last long enough to cause a severe falloff in new truck sales. The overall truck market for 1920 sank to 179,000 units, and Ford sales tumbled to 43,934 units. The second year of the depression, 1921, saw the truck market total drop even further, to just under 121,000 trucks, while Ford sales managed to bounce back to 67,796.

Early that same year, William "Big Bill" Knudsen, the Ford production executive who'd overseen construction of the Rouge and had set up an entire network of Ford assembly plants across the country, tendered his resignation effective February 1921. He and another Ford executive by the name of Charles Sorensen had been battling for some time, both trying to become Mr. Ford's favorite, and the big Dane finally decided the

An example of a fairly typical Ford delivery truck is this 1924 Model T fitted with an enclosed body and cab used by the Century Floral Shop in downtown Detroit for flower delivery. The sliding-door body and cab were probably made by Martin-Parry. Notice the higher hood line on this truck, a styling feature introduced this year.

stress wasn't worth it. Before long General Motors recruited him, and he was soon put in charge of its Chevrolet division. Determined to grow the Chevy passenger car and truck business in a big way, Knudsen inspired dealers with his famous promise to match Ford's production rate "one for one," though with his thick Danish accent it came out as "vun for vun." To accomplish that goal would be an enormous task; at the time Ford was outselling Chevrolet by a factor of fourteen to one in passenger cars, and sixteen to one in trucks. In fact, among GM's highest officers there had been talk of dropping Chevrolet, though with Knudsen now on board they had high hopes for the future. Knudsen was probably the top production man in the world and if anybody could make Chevy prosper, he could.

Also during 1921, the Dodge Brothers Company (less the brothers themselves; they both passed away in 1920) became the sole distributors of products of the Graham Brothers' truck company. The Dodge firm would eventually purchase Graham Brothers, which in time would greatly expand the Dodge truck portfolio. It is interesting to pause here to note that Ford's two largest competitors, Chevrolet and Dodge, were in effect "encouraged" by Henry Ford. Chevrolet's rise would come about because of Knudsen's efforts, while Dodge was created when the Dodge Brothers went out on their own as carmakers.

For a time the Ford Motor Company itself faced sharp financial difficulties when the short depression aggravated a fiscal squeeze resulting from Mr. Ford's efforts to buy out the company's other shareholders. When the 1920 to 1921 depression began, Ford found himself short of cash, and it was touch and go for a while as he conferred with bankers

Although this is a 1924 Model T truck, it has the C-style cab, wherein the windshield, curved roof, and side doors are the driver's main protection against the elements. In really cold weather, plastic side curtain windows could be installed, and if so equipped, the heater could be used to warm up the cab. This light express body h as a canopy roof with roll-down sides.

and Wall Street investment houses in an effort to secure the working capital his company desperately needed. Apparently Ford even gave thought to selling some company stock to the public, but in the end he was able to solve his cash problems by pressuring his dealers to take more cars and trucks than they needed. This alleviated the capital shortage until the new car market bounced back.

With sufficient capital now at hand and a strong market returning, Ford Motor Company was able to nearly double its trucks sales in 1922, to more than 127,000 units in the United States, its greatest year ever to that point. This was the dominant position in the market by far; second place Dodge sold about 22,000 trucks, while third place REO sold 14,854 units. However, six years earlier Dodge had not even been a factor in the truck market, so it was obviously moving up. Chevrolet sold about 7,100 trucks for 1922 but was preparing to launch a major assault on the truck segment.

Electric starting and lighting were now optionally available on the Ford truck chassis, which added greatly to their appeal; after all, no one really cared to stand out in the rain and cold trying to crank-start their trucks. And everyone knew that electric lighting was much better than gas or oil lamps. Closed cabs (sometimes called four-season cabs) were also starting to gain favor. They were more costly to buy, but having one meant that drivers could work longer hours and travel greater distances in relative comfort. Steel was replacing wood in body panel construction, though it would be a long while before metal replaced wood entirely. Still, progress was being made.

Another 1924 Ford truck, this one is built on the 1-ton Model TT chassis, which is easily identified by the large rear wheels and tires. The stake body with rack sides was useful for most hauling jobs and the C side cab could be fitted with winter enclosures to protect the driver.

This truck is identified as a 1925 Model T, but it is obviously a Model TT and was photographed at the same time as the photo on the left because the same car can be seen in the background of both photos. Thus it's probably a 1924 model fitted with a screen-side delivery body.

A RECORD YEAR

The following year, 1923, Ford Motor Company reached another new peak in production when it built over two million vehicles. US retail sales of Ford trucks climbed to 193,234 units. Despite a respectable increase in sales, Dodge trucks slipped to third place with 28,652 trucks delivered. The new number two was Chevrolet, which retailed 30,985 trucks. Even REO did well, despite its emphasis on larger vehicles, selling 17,646 trucks. International Harvester, which sold only in the heavier ranges, delivered over 10,000 units for 1923.

Part of Ford's success was due to its ability to offer financing, the rest was mainly due to its huge retail network and first-in-mind brand recognition because, truth be told, the company still offered only two basic truck types, the Model T chassis and the Model TT chassis. While it's true that literally dozens of truck body types were available, covering nearly every sort of industry and use, the company had nothing to offer in the 2-, 3-, or 4-ton range. A few enterprising outside firms began to offer up fitted TT chassis rated for much heavier loads, but there was a limit to how high they could go with cargo weight because the standard Ford engine produced just 20 horsepower at 1,500 rpm. Because of the low-power engines in use in the early days of the industry, trucks usually traveled very slowly. But as roads continued to be improved and markets continued to open up all across the land, businesses and farmers were becoming more interested in trucks that could travel at higher speeds. It boiled down to the old saying "time is money."

Ford continued to build up its production capacity in 1923 in anticipation of even greater sales volumes and began construction on a new engineering laboratory in Dearborn, Michigan, which would be used for crafting improvements to existing products and investigating new products as well. Up to this point, the Ford research activities had been a bit helter-skelter, but now they would be formalized in a brand-new, state-of-the-art facility. That could only be good news for Ford buyers.

The Roaring Twenties roared on. For 1924 Ford returned with the same Model T- and Model TT-based trucks with minor improvements. During the year the company produced its ten millionth automobile, an amazing record considering the age and size of the industry. Ford was clearly the largest auto and truck company in the world, with even mighty General Motors appearing small in comparison. But to many buyers, the Model T was beginning to look a little old, as was the Model TT. More modern vehicles were coming on the market now, though because of their smaller production volumes they were invariably priced higher than the Ford. In addition, Ford cars and trucks were known as sturdy, well-built vehicles and their service network was the envy of the world. So despite their growing age, Fords still had a lot to offer.

ABOVE: Here we can see several 1925 Ford trucks owned by the Detroit Gas Company, including both T and TT models. First in line is what appears to be a TT with either a dump body or express body. The last two appear to be Model Ts with express bodies.

RIGHT: James Cargo Wholesale was the owner of this 1925 Model T roadster pickup. Although it was a sturdy worker, one can see its limitations for load carrying—notice the cargo hanging off the back. Still, the Model T pickup was a light, dependable, and inexpensive delivery vehicle.

A COMPLETE TRUCK

If there was one thing Henry Ford was sure of, it was this: he wanted to control the manufacture of his products—and all the parts and components they were made of—himself. In its early days, the Ford Motor Company was content to farm out the manufacture of many parts to outside suppliers, but that business model had been born of necessity. As soon as the company was able to, it began to shift parts production to its own plants. By the early 1920s the Ford plant was probably the most integrated production facility in the world. However, when it came to trucks, the company still generally provided only the chassis and cowl, because the wide array of truck body types the market demanded wasn't easily accommodated with Ford's mass production methods. But during the 1924 model year Ford made a major announcement to its dealers; it would thenceforth supply truck bodies as well as chassis. The announcement came in October 1923, and the first type provided was an all-steel express truck body shipped to dealers in component form.

This 1925 photo is labeled as a Model T, but it is actually a TT with a C-style cab enclosure and light express body. Both the Model T and TT were given improved engine lubrication systems this year as well as lighter-weight pistons to reduce reciprocating mass. Improvements were also made to the steering system on both models.

Prices Too High?
We'll Lower Them!

Part of Ford's success must be credited to its manufacturing efficiency, which allowed it
to reduce prices substantially; the 1922 Model T chassis was priced at $295, while the
Model TT was now $390. Such affordable prices were a major draw, and in addition to the
major success Ford had in the US market, overseas sales of Ford truck chassis also climbed.
Even more important though was a marked return to prosperity in the country. The US economy
took off, and with factories turning out millions of new consumer products, there was a huge
demand for trucks to move those products to market, along with trucks for home builders, road
and bridge construction, and home deliveries of coal, oil, milk, and bread. It was at this point
that the Roaring Twenties really began to roar. Ford also managed to sell more than
a million cars during the year, and in February purchased the Lincoln Motor
Company in order to expand into other automobile industry segments.

It was the dealer's responsibility to then assemble the body on the chassis. A canopy top was soon made available as well, and in January 1924 a Ford-designed open cab was finally offered with a roof, windshield, rear section, and doors but otherwise open on the C-shaped sides. Plastic side curtains could be fitted to provide protection from the elements. The price for a new 1-ton chassis with express body and cab was reportedly $490. Options included oil lamps, oversized tires, and the canopy top. The company soon had eight distinct combinations of commercial body/chassis available, which meant it was now easier for dealers to order trucks. However, due to the vast range of body types needed in industry and farming, there were still plenty of opportunities for independent truck body firms to market their own products.

The Ford trucks came in for some minor styling changes this year, with a higher radiator and hood being the most noticeable. School bus bodies mounted on TT chassis were becoming more and more common, as were enclosed-cab delivery bodies.

For the 1924 calendar year Ford sold 172,221 trucks, down from the record-setting prior year but an amazing number all the same. Dodge rose to second place in industry sales with just over 31,000 trucks retailed.

Ford introduced additional new truck types for 1925, beginning with a platform stake truck announced in December 1924. A closed-cab body became available in the spring and could be purchased with most of the commercial body types. Ford also introduced a factory-built light-duty pickup truck when it announced the "Model T Runabout with Pickup Body" in April 1925. This consisted of a Model T runabout with a factory-installed all-steel pickup bed. The bed itself was 56 inches long, 40.75 inches wide, and 13 inches tall, and it included four stake pockets and an adjustable tailgate. Priced at just $281 and perfect for light loads, more than 33,000 were sold during the year.

Both the Model T and Model TT received mechanical improvements this year that included improved engine lubrication systems along with lighter-weight pistons to reduce reciprocating mass. Improvements were also made to the steering system.

During 1925 Ford Motor Company produced its twelve millionth car and one millionth truck. Ford truck sales eclipsed every record in the books, with more than 268,000 units sold in the United States. By this time reportedly 75 percent of all the 1-ton trucks on America's roads were Fords. However, both Dodge and Chevrolet also saw big sales gains for 1925, and they seemed to be building momentum.

TROUBLE ON THE HORIZON

In spite of the enormous sales volumes in the prior year, as the 1926 model year began many officials at the Ford Motor Company were worried about falling passenger car sales. Deliveries of Ford Model T cars had peaked in 1924 at 1.4 million vehicles, then dropped to 1.25 million the following year, even as Chevrolet sales continued to rise. The trend line for 1926 seemed to indicate a further decline in Ford car sales was coming. Even sales of Ford trucks now appeared to be slipping.

The root cause of all of this was not a declining market but rather an increasing sophistication on the part of vehicle buyers. In the early days of the industry, when many people were buying their first car or truck, they were naturally in the dark as to exactly what to expect performance-wise. But now with the auto market beginning to mature, people were

For light-duty use, the Model T roadster pickup was always a good choice. Note the higher hood line introduced earlier on the series. This is a 1926 model. By this point, sales of the Model T cars and trucks were falling off, a result of increased competition from Chevrolet and Willys-Overland.

becoming more sophisticated and aware of the advantages and disadvantages of certain automotive features. Many people were now buying their second or third vehicle and they knew a lot more about mechanical features than they once did. As sturdy as they were, the Models T and TT were hampered by an antiquated 2-speed planetary transmission, while most competitors offered the more advanced sliding gear transmission with three or four speeds. In addition, the Fords were seen as under-powered. Roads were improving and people now wanted faster, more powerful cars and trucks, and in this regard Ford was falling behind the rest of the automotive pack. All of this was having a negative impact on sales, and with thirty-six assembly plants spitting out cars and trucks, that was a big worry. Many Ford executives recognized the problem, but whenever they suggested to old Henry that it might be time to design a replacement for his beloved Model T, Ford would become enraged, declaring that the T would go on as it was forever. Cussedly stubborn, he refused to listen to anyone who spoke against the Model T.

Besides the mechanical aspects, buyers were also looking for a bit more comfort and luxury than before, and styling was beginning to become an important sales feature even in the low-priced market. The spindly black Model T looked dated next to a bright new Willys or Chevrolet, and many people were now willing to spend a few dollars extra to get a little more style. Here Henry proved a bit more flexible and for 1926 Ford cars and Model T light trucks featured handsome new body styling. Radiators and hoods were raised and their lines now mated smoothly with a restyled cowl. New fenders and wider running boards debuted. The styling changes were not introduced on the TT series trucks, however, probably on the theory that a truck is a truck and its appearance and styling were unimportant.

Ford Truck Display

STAKE BODY · · · · · · · ONE TON

A light-weight truck for farm use and general utility purposes. Stakes are in six sets, enclosing sides and both ends, easily removable to provide flat platform. Can be equipped with cattle and grain sides, or cross boards. With open style of cab cost is $20 less.

$515⁰⁰

F. O. B. DETROIT

RUNABOUT · · · · PICK-UP BODY

INCLUDING STARTER AND DEMOUNTABLE RIMS—For light pick-up work, and speedy delivery of parcels, produce, groceries, etc. An all-steel body, 40¾ by 56 inches, replaces the rear deck of the standard Model T Ford runabout. Adjustable rear gate.

$366⁰⁰

F. O. B. DETROIT

AUTHORIZED Ford Dealers, throughout the United States, will make a special display next week of Ford Trucks and Ford-built Bodies. Dependable low cost trucking units—100% Ford value—built complete to Ford standards of serviceability are available for almost every type of haulage and delivery.

Over a million of these Ford Trucks and light delivery cars are in service today—giving dependable and economical service to their users. Chassis and body alike possess those in-built qualities of strength and durability that are identified with all Ford products. Exceptional quality of materials and workmanship has been possible because of the huge

Week - July 13ᵀᴴ to 18ᵀᴴ

A full line of *Ford-built* bodies on the sturdy *Ford* chassis

❦ ❦ ❦

volume of Ford production. And it is the economies of this large-scale production which permit selling these complete trucking units—Ford Trucks and Ford Bodies—at such remarkably low prices.

You can secure any type of Standard Ford-built Body with either closed or open steel cab. Your nearest Authorized Ford Dealer invites you to visit his display room next week and make careful inspection of these complete low-cost Ford trucking units. Or, phone the dealer the particular type of truck or commercial car you are interested in and he will be glad to drive it to your door for a demonstration.

Ford Motor Company
DETROIT

TRUCKS
AND DELIVERY CARS

EXPRESS BODY · · · · CLOSED CAB

$505.00
F. O. B. DETROIT

For general hauling and delivery service of one-ton loads under hard conditions of service. Body of all-steel construction. Loading space, 7 feet, 2 inches by 4 feet. Stake sockets are provided for side boards, racks, canopy, etc. With open cab, $485.00 f. o. b. Detroit.

EXPRESS BODY WITH CANOPY TOP · OPEN CAB

$515.00
F. O. B. DETROIT

Particularly adapted to the use of wholesale and commission houses, and for general delivery purposes. All-steel body as in express type. Roof and curtains of durable, weather-proof materials. Curtains easily raised or lowered. With closed cab, $535.00 f. o. b. Detroit.

EXPRESS BODY WITH SCREEN SIDES · CLOSED CAB

$560.00
F. O. B. DETROIT

Widely used for package delivery by department stores, express companies, etc., also manufacturers' pick-up purposes. All-steel express body. Rear screens lock securely. Curtains for weather protection. Loading space 48" x 86". With open cab, $540.00 f. o. b. Detroit.

ABOVE: This 1926 Ford Model TT stake truck is a real beauty, with its enclosed cab, big windows, and large stake body with racks installed.

RIGHT: The Model T shown here is being used as a jitney bus and is obviously overloaded to a shocking degree. However, the tough little Ford could handle more abuse than most people could throw at it and keep plugging along. That's one of the reasons why Americans loved their Ford vehicles—they were built to last.

Ford truck sales continued to drop during 1926, falling to just over 200,000 units. Meanwhile Chevrolet sales climbed to 55,000 trucks, though Dodge sales plummeted to just 24,000, with Graham adding another 24,800 to the total. Heavy-truck specialist International Harvester sold 13,535 units in the United States.

Faced with a continuing falloff in sales, Henry Ford eventually admitted he needed to develop something new, and thus the Ford Motor Company announced during 1927 that it was preparing an all-new passenger car for introduction sometime later in the year. Here, though, Henry Ford made one of the worst mistakes in automotive history. He shut down production of the Model T in midyear in order to finish working out preparations for the new car. For months no Ford cars would be produced in his massive factories, although the Model TT trucks continued in production through the summer. This incredibly shortsighted act allowed Chevrolet to surpass Ford in both car and truck sales for the year. General Motors had been laboring for years to beat Ford, but in 1927 Ford handed the low-price sales crown to Chevrolet on a platter. Ford truck sales totaled just 99,451 while Chevrolet sold 104,832.

Henry Ford and his able engineers went to work developing and tooling up for the all-new Ford cars and trucks while Henry's son Edsel worked with a small team to create new styling that would make Ford among the most handsome vehicles on the road. In doing so, it appears that they took the contemporary Lincoln as their inspiration. That ended up being a good move.

In undertaking to field an entirely new line of vehicles, the Ford Motor Company was choosing to turn its face to the future rather than remain stuck in the past. And the vehicles that were to result from this mighty effort would become legendary.

Chapter 3

FORD EXPANDS

Henry and Edsel Ford proudly introduced their all-new automobile in December 1927 as a 1928 model in what would be the company's twenty-fifth year in business. In naming it the Model A, a designation he used years earlier, Henry Ford explained that the new car was so different from the Model T that he felt he needed to start his model identification system all over again at the beginning of the alphabet. Of course, it may simply have been a case of Henry realizing that "Model U" didn't really slip off the tongue easily.

The Model A closed-cab pickup for 1929. Note the black fenders and wheels, as well as the composite top. In this era, truck roofs were often made of rubber or a rubberized composite material. The easiest way to spot a Model A is to look for the gas cap on the cowl.

The new Model A Fords were extremely nice automobiles with fine-car styling; a more powerful 40-horsepower, 200.5-cubic-inch, four-cylinder engine (twice the output of the Model T); a 3-speed sliding gear transmission; and important improvements to ride and handling. Millions of people flocked to Ford showrooms to see them.

The passenger cars were soon joined by completely new trucks sharing many body and mechanical parts with the car line. The light-truck line, based on the Model A's 103.5-inch wheelbase, initially consisted of just a commercial chassis and a roadster pickup, but other models were soon added. The heavy-duty line, now designated the AA, also went into production. Substantially upgraded, it rode a heavier-duty frame with a 131.5-inch wheelbase and carried a nominal rating of 1½ tons. Naturally, front and rear springs were heavier duty than before, and a stronger rear axle and two-piece driveshaft were also included. The four-wheel brake system included a parking brake, and the 20-inch welded steel spoke wheels were fitted with heavy-duty tires. Initially the AA chassis was priced at $460, though that was increased by springtime to $540—still an excellent value.

Even lower priced was the 1928 Model A roadster pickup seen here; it was tagged at a mere $395! The roadster pickup was actually the first factory-built pickup manufactured by Ford; the closed-cab pickup was introduced some weeks later.

During 1928 a panel truck and a closed-cab pickup joined the line; however, it appears that because of high demand, these body types were reserved first for the AA line before being offered in the lighter series in August. Platform bodies were also available for the AA line and could be ordered with the stake-side option, grain-side option, or various rack bodies. Naturally, popular bodies, such as the express, continued to be offered. New-style bus bodies soon were available as well to make use of the AA's powerful engine and greater capacity. Ford itself offered a standard nine-passenger bus body for the A series and a fourteen-passenger bus on the AA chassis, while outside builders offered a broad array of bus bodies for the AA. These same suppliers also introduced new higher-capacity dump bodies. To help handle these larger loads, a new 2-speed gear set was optional; it provided six forward speeds, meaning that the new Ford trucks could not only carry more, but they could travel at higher speeds as well.

The new Model A closed-cab pickup was one of the handsomest trucks on the road, and with a price tag of just $445, a tremendous value as well. Even so, sales of Ford trucks for 1928 fell to a reported 61,985, probably due to problems getting the production lines up to full capacity along with the company's emphasis on turning out as many passenger cars as possible. Chevrolet, on an upward path since 1925, sold over 133,000 trucks for 1928, more than twice Ford's total.

Not to worry. By year-end things at Ford Motor Company were running smoother and management began to turn up the dial on production. With the stock market roaring and prosperity reigning throughout the land, everyone was certain that sales during 1929 would see a great improvement. They were right. In fact, the 1929 model year would shatter all industry records for both cars and trucks.

Ford Motor Company took several important steps to increase its trucks sales for 1929, beginning with a big boost in production output. The company also introduced

Here we see another 1929 Ford truck, this one with a special enclosed van body built for US Postal Service usage. Ford produced thousands of delivery trucks each year during this period.

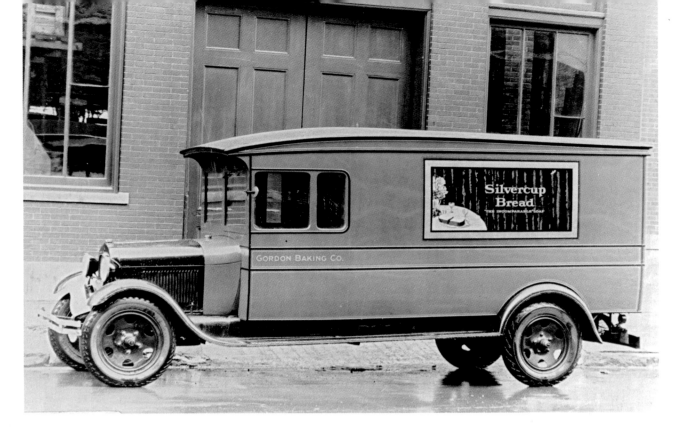

additional commercial models in both the A and AA series in hopes of enticing more buyers. New this year was the deluxe delivery car, a two-door Ford Model A with no rear seat, blanked-out rear side windows, and a side-hinged door at the rear for easy access to its cargo compartment. Priced at $595, it could carry a decent-sized load with complete weather protection. Bigger news was the introduction of the industry's first assembly-line-produced station wagon. In that era station wagons were considered commercial vehicles, thus their inclusion in the truck line rather than the car line. The new wagon was a beauty, boasting Ford Model A front-end sheet metal mated to an all-wood four-door wagon body constructed by coachbuilder Murray Corporation. Made of hard maple with birch paneling, it was an elegant vehicle that proved quite popular with hotels and resorts that purchased them to convey guests. The new wagon was priced at a very reasonable $695.

Ford also introduced numerous running changes to its vehicles during 1928 and 1929. One important change was a switch to disc-type steel wheels on the AA series beginning around February. Toward the end of the year a 4-speed transmission was made standard equipment on AAs, a welcome addition because it provided greater pulling power at low speeds. Along the way suspensions were beefed up, as were both front and rear axles and front brakes.

The sales picture for 1929 turned out to be as good as any could have hoped for, with industry truck sales rising to just over 490,000 units, of which the Ford Motor Company accounted for 212,254, edging out Chevrolet, which sold 160,959 trucks. Third-place International sold nearly 30,000 trucks. Total industry sales of cars and trucks topped 4.3 million units, smashing the old record by more than 800,000 vehicles.

This 1929 Model AA bread truck appears to be built on an extended chassis. By this time most trucks were being produced with enclosed cabs for driver comfort and safety. Ford boosted truck production dramatically this year.

UH OH, TROUBLE COMING

In September 1929, stock prices on Wall Street began to fall. Initially this was thought to be a normal and to-be-expected market correction because, in truth, the market had been overheated for far too long. But day after day, stocks continued to edge downward at a worrisome pace and on October 29—a day that would later be referred to as Black Tuesday—prices suddenly plummeted and thousands of investors were wiped out. Thus began a long, dark period in our nation's history known as the Great Depression. No one could know that it would be many years before vehicle sales would again reach the heights set earlier in 1929.

Meanwhile Ford was readying its 1930 trucks for sale. Styling updates introduced on passenger cars in January 1930 made for an even more handsome automobile than before, though it was quite a while before they were fully incorporated into the truck lines. Changes were made to the cowl, fenders, radiator shell, and bumpers. Hoods were raised and new headlamps introduced as well. By June 1930 the transformation was mostly complete and

A particularly handsome rig is this 1929 Model AA stake-side, purchased by the M.D. Moffitt Tile Company of Long Beach, California. Loads of tile are quite heavy, so Mr. Moffitt was smart to choose the heavier-duty AA over a less expensive A. Note the heavy-duty steel wheels.

PREVIOUS PAGES: Here is a 1930 Model AA dump truck with dual rear wheels for extra carrying capacity and strength. Ford began offering a line of factory-supplied dump trucks in July 1930. This small 1.5-cubic-yard model was the least expensive dump truck in the new lineup.

LEFT: Although the 1930 Model A roadster pickup—sometimes referred to as an open-cab pickup—featured some neat styling updates this year, the day of the open pickup had already passed and only 3,429 were produced for 1930.

BELOW: Here we see the shorter-wheelbase version of the Model AA, which is also equipped with taller side racks. This is a platform stake body with what were called "cattle racks" mounted on a 131.5-inch AA chassis. The bottom part of the box could be used to haul grain. To haul cattle the 5-foot side racks could be added in a few moments, or left on year-round.

a third chassis joined the truck line, a longer AA on a 157-inch wheelbase. To differentiate between the two AA models, the original was now called the AA-131 while the new one was called the AA-157. Although some thought was given to also adding a longer-wheelbase A truck model, in the end it wasn't produced.

At about the same time as the appearance of new styling updates came an all-new express body for the AA-131, as well as a new panel truck body. New stake, platform, and express bodies to fit the AA-157 were likewise introduced. Outside suppliers also introduced a wide variety of larger van, bus, and express bodies to fit the longer chassis.

Although industry sales fell during 1930, a result of the worsening economic situation, it ended up being a decent year for the Ford Motor Company, all things considered. Its dealers retailed more than 177,000 trucks and more than a million passenger cars, once again making Ford number one in industry sales in both cars and trucks. Chevrolet took second place in truck sales, managing to retail a bit over 118,000 trucks that year while third-place International sold nearly 20,000 units. The great disparity between second and third place can be easily explained; at this point International Harvester

This 1931 Model A closed-cab pickup is an ultra-rare Type 66-A Deluxe Pickup. This was a new model this year and featured a bed design that was more integrated with the cab. Offered only with the enclosed cab, the Deluxe didn't prove popular among buyers and only a reported 293 were produced, with most of them going to General Electric as part of a refrigerator promotion.

De Luxe Delivery   *Town-Car Delivery*

De Luxe Delivery Units at Ford low cost

Now, every merchant, every store, and every business which offers a delivery-service can enjoy the added prestige that comes of operating smart and handsome delivery-units. There are several such de luxe types in the standard Ford line, completely appointed and equipped . . . but priced well within reach of any operator.

The *town-car delivery* is a final step in distinctive appearance. This is a car for the boulevard and avenue, one perfectly at home in any assemblage of smart motor cars. The front seat is upholstered in black genuine leather. The spacious loading compartment, of ample proportions, is finished with veneer panels in natural color. Six steel-spoke wheels, two fender-wells, an ornamental light on each side, two dome-lights and an extension-mirror are standard equipment.

Other handsome units take care of a wide variety of delivery require-

ments. The *de luxe delivery* is used by many druggists, specialty grocers, caterers, jewelers, silversmiths, stationers, florists, and others who need a fully enclosed unit of good capacity.

The *de luxe panel truck* is designed for the larger load. The *de luxe pickup* is a favorite choice with those who need an open delivery unit for carrying high-grade merchandise.

Because the de luxe appointments are standard equipment, these Ford units are unusually low in cost. Durable materials and rugged construction throughout, and low gasoline and oil consumption make them economical to maintain and operate.

Your Ford dealer will be glad to help you in your delivery problems. In most principal cities, there are centralized exhibits of Ford trucks and light commercial cars.

De Luxe Panel Truck   *De Luxe Pickup*

still didn't offer any models in the light-truck market (i.e., ½-ton or ¾-ton models), and that was where the volume sales were. There was also interesting news overseas: this year Ford Model AA trucks went into production in the Soviet Union at a big plant in Moscow. It seems capitalist Henry Ford was quite a hero in Russia, where he was viewed as a friend to the working man. And anyway, Joseph Stalin needed trucks for his big "cooperative" farms.

The following year, 1931, saw an even steeper decline in the American economy. Industry sales of trucks and passenger cars sank to their lowest level since 1922 as business activities everywhere continued to dry up. The Ford Model A automobile was now in its fourth year of production and got hit particularly hard with sales falling about 50 percent. Thankfully truck sales held up better, though dropping to roughly 125,000 units.

The sales falloff wasn't the fault of the truck makers—Ford and its rivals were building some of their best trucks ever. The problem was simply that the economy continued to worsen, and by now even the most optimistic souls were worried. There were hungry people standing in bread lines in every major city, thousands of companies had gone out of business, and the situation seemed to only get worse with each passing month.

Ford introduced more than a dozen new body styles for trucks during 1931, including a stylish deluxe pickup with a more integrated-appearing pickup bed on the Model A chassis with a closed cab. Regular A-model pickups also got a new bed design, not quite as stylish but very serviceable. Produced by Briggs Manufacturing Company, these newly designed As could handle larger loads than before and were available in a canopy top version as well. Also new was a special delivery body made of natural-finish wood similar to the station wagon, though with closed sides and only two doors rather than four. Several new panel truck bodies were added to the line during the year, as well as new ambulance types. Summer 1931 brought a new stand-and-drive model that was popular with firms that delivered bakery or dairy goods door-to-door.

Tractor-trailer combinations had become common by this time, but Ford was beginning to lag a bit behind its competitors because it still produced only four-cylinder trucks. Although the Ford trucks could be geared to haul heavy loads, doing so tended to restrict their top speed. Other companies were offering hefty six-cylinder engines that were smoother and more powerful than the Ford four-banger and that was being reflected in the sales charts. Undeterred, Henry was working on a solution that would be introduced for the 1932 models.

1932

What to do? The economy was in a slump, car and truck sales were down dramatically, and the outlook wasn't good. Ford, once the king of automakers, was falling behind General Motors, which offered a slate of six-cylinder low-priced cars and trucks through their Chevrolet Division. Ford needed to come up with a more competitive engine. But what sort should it be? In the end, a jealous Henry Ford decreed that his cars and trucks would be powered by a V-8 engine. Nothing less would do.

If Six is Good, Eight Must Be Better

The problem Henry Ford faced was this: since 1929 Chevrolet had offered buyers a more powerful six-cylinder engine, having dropped its four-cylinder, and this was luring thousands of customers away from Ford products. Sixes had once been the reserve of medium-priced automobiles and heavy-duty trucks and to be able to offer a six for about the same price as a four was a huge enticement. Henry needed to respond to this threat, but he believed that introducing a six in his vehicles would make him appear to be following GM rather than leading the market, as he'd always done. So he set his mind to bringing out something that would outshine the Chevrolet offerings. If six cylinders were good, he reasoned, then eight cylinders were even better—and so that's what Ford decided it would be.

Up to this point, eight-cylinder engines had been used almost exclusively in higher priced cars and in most cases they were big, heavy inline motors. Most of the V-8s that had appeared utilized multipiece blocks due to the difficulty of trying to cast a one-piece block. But Ford decided his new engine would be a compact V-8 with a one-piece block, which would reduce weight and costs considerably. His engineers had a miserable time working out the production process, but eventually they did, and the new mill was introduced in late March 1932. Displacing 221 cubic inches, the Ford V-8 produced 65 horsepower, a notable improvement over the 40-horsepower Model A engine. Like prior Ford engines, the new V-8 was a flathead design.

Realizing that some buyers might worry about the V-8's fuel economy, Ford decided to offer a choice of powerplants. He had his four-cylinder engine reworked and upgraded to 50 horsepower. This was installed in a completely new chassis with a 106-inch wheelbase, dubbed the Ford Model B. V-8-powered models were designated the Model 18 (which reportedly stood for "first eight"), B-18, or simply the Ford V-8. Initially the V-8 engines were reserved for passenger cars, but in time the company began installing them in light trucks as well. By fall the V-8 was also being installed in the heavy-duty trucks, where their greater power was most needed. The price difference between the four-cylinder and eight-cylinder models was about fifty dollars.

Bodies for 1932 were all new, made entirely of steel, and featured a rear-mounted fuel tank, finally getting rid of the A's in-your-lap cowl-mounted tank. A new synchromesh transmission was also introduced.

Naturally the new chassis and wheelbase called for new commercial bodies. Most of these were designed along the lines of the previous bodies, so they included panel truck, van, delivery, pickup, stake, and rack types. Some existing bodies, however, didn't have enough sales volume to warrant a redesign and were dropped, including the fancy deluxe pickup and the natural-wood delivery.

The 1932 Ford Model B roadster pickup (shown here) was a rare sight even in 1932 because demand had shrunk so low that reportedly less than six hundred units were produced that year.

A new heavy-duty chassis also appeared, dubbed the BB. As with the previous heavy-duty chassis, this one was rated at a 1½-ton capacity and rode the same wheelbases used previously: 131 and 157 inches. A sturdy new frame featured 7-inch deep frame rails and semi-elliptic rear springs.

Vehicle production delays that were caused by problems getting sufficient V-8 engines produced by launch time, along with a worsening economy that bottomed out that year, caused Ford sales to fall sharply for 1932, with just 60,234 trucks retailed. Chevrolet light-truck sales also slumped, though they managed to outsell Ford by the slimmest of margins. International sold 13,232 trucks that same year. Although these were dismal sales results, by year-end there were signs that the economy was beginning to slowly crawl back from the brink and businessmen everywhere were hopeful that the roots of a recovery were starting to take hold.

Booze Helps

America's great experiment in outlawing alcoholic beverages throughout the nation ended during 1933 when the Volstead Act (a.k.a. Prohibition) was repealed. Distilleries, long inactive or producing alcohol only for medical or commercial purposes, shifted into high gear, ramping up production of beverage alcohol. As a direct result of this, farmers began planting millions more acres of the grains used in distilling spirits and quickly found they needed to purchase more trucks to handle the large volume of new business coming their way. Distilleries needed more trucks to move the merchandise to stores. The economy in general began to come out of its long slumber, though tens of thousands of Americans remained on relief. Overall, however, the signs were encouraging. Things were beginning to look up.

Ford had something notable to celebrate in 1933: its thirtieth year in business. The company shocked the industry that February when it debuted new cars and light trucks on a new chassis with an X-member frame, 6-inch-longer wheelbase, and completely new styling. The all-steel bodies looked much more modern, even aerodynamic, with styling that matched the trends of the time and were extremely handsome. However, in regards to the truck line, the new styling was carried over only to car-based light-duty models, such as the sedan delivery, ambulance, station wagon, and hearse models. Larger vehicles, such as panel trucks, stand-drives, vans, deliveries, and heavy-duty units, continued to use the older-style bodies. The reason for this was that the truck market was continuing to evolve, and the day when trucks and automobiles could share bodies was drawing to a close. Car styling was becoming lower, less utilitarian, and more aerodynamic, all of which made automobile bodies less suitable for use in truck lines. In addition, the passenger car market had become so competitive that model changes needed to be introduced fairly often, whereas lower-volume trucks could soldier on with older styling and not have to go through the expensive retooling process that passenger cars required. Most companies felt it wasn't cost-effective.

For 1933 Ford again offered both four- and eight-cylinder truck models. The light-duty commercial cars were exceedingly handsome, but some buyers were put off by reports that the Ford V-8 suffered from excessive oil and gas consumption. Some chose to purchase the four-cylinder Ford instead, but many who would not settle for a four-cylinder vehicle ended up buying a competitor's product instead.

During the year the company produced its twenty-one millionth Ford, a remarkable achievement by any measure. On the downside, Ford was outsold in the light-truck market during 1933, retailing just 56,157 units to Chevy's 99,880. Dodge, launching an all-out attempt to gain market share, sold over 25,000 trucks. International also had an excellent year, with sales climbing to over 22,000 vehicles, a result of finally offering light pickup models in the ½-ton range.

1934–1935: TURNAROUND

For the 1935 model year, Ford restyled its trucks and the new look was quite modern and attractive. The basic styling was carried over to the 1936 models, including this sharp little V-8 pickup. This year the company proudly celebrated production of the three millionth Ford truck, as well as production of the three millionth V-8 engine.

Ford introduced minor updates and improvements to its truck lines in 1934. The BB series was given a new full-floating rear axle this year, and standard equipment was upgraded. The biggest changes were improvements made to the V-8 engine to fix some ongoing mechanical problems and make it more durable. The one millionth Ford V-8 engine was produced this year. As the V-8 grew in popularity, more and more transit companies began ordering school and passenger buses on the Ford chassis. During the year the company discontinued offering the four-cylinder engine in commercial cars built for the US market, though the four remained available for overseas sales. This year was also the last time the open cab pickups were offered, and reference sources claim that less than four hundred units were produced for the year.

With a steadily improving economy, Ford was able to more than double its truck sales for 1934 and had an excellent year with passenger cars as well. The automotive industry as a whole showed a nice increase, not as high percentage-wise as the year before, but the upswing provided further evidence that the worst of the Depression was behind them. Americans everywhere began to have more hope for the future.

The turnaround in the American economy continued to grow in strength as the 1935 model year began. Ford restyled its passenger cars once again, this time with the engine and transmission moved forward in the chassis in order that all passengers would be riding between the axles, which resulted in a greatly improved ride quality. For the most part the light commercial car line, the Model 50, shared in the chassis changes, which resulted in less rear overhang because the distance from the cab to the rear axle was reduced. In most cases overall length was also less. Stylish new cabs debuted for both the Model 50 series and the 1½-ton Model 51. The heavy-duty chassis also received some important upgrades, including improvements in the frame, brakes, and suspension.

A company called Transportation Engineers Inc. of Highland Park, Michigan, introduced a new cab-over engine adaptation of the Ford chassis, as did a few other firms. These units were useful in states with laws on the books restricting how long commercial truck-trailer combinations could be.

FOUR-WHEEL DRIVE, ANYONE?

Even more notable, the Marmon-Herrington Company of Indianapolis announced a new all-wheel-drive Ford truck, a four-wheel-drive conversion of the Ford heavy-duty chassis. These rugged units would prove useful in plowing, construction, farming, and eventually military use.

At the end of 1935 the Ford Motor Company could congratulate itself. The company not only greatly increased its truck sales volume, but it also recaptured first place among automobile brands, selling a total of more than 826,000 passenger cars and 161,000 trucks. Neither total was as high as in 1930 but nevertheless marked an outstanding comeback from the sad days of the Great Depression.

Vernor's is a soda company that originated in the Detroit area and happily is still in business all these years later. Famous for its delicious ginger ale, Vernors's management seems to have long favored Ford trucks. Shown here is a 1936 stake truck.

1936–1937

Having introduced so much that was new for 1935, Ford decided to carryover most of its products for 1936. Further modifications were made to improve cooling because the V-8 still had a tendency to run hot. Light-duty commercial cars, designated the Model 67, continued to share much sheet metal with Ford passenger cars. That said, the range of Ford truck models and body options for 1936 was almost bewildering. In addition to such passenger-car-based models as the sedan delivery and station wagons, there were panel trucks, box vans, pickups, stand-and-drives, platform trucks, armored cars, rack bodies, dump bodies, oil trucks, coal trucks, plow trucks, fire trucks, grain bodies, stake trucks, buses of every type imaginable, and tractor-trailer combos. Added to that were the cowl-and-chassis models, cab-and-chassis models, and stripped chassis.

During 1936 the company proudly celebrated production of the three millionth Ford truck, as well as production of the three millionth V-8 engine. However, sales of cars and trucks fell that year as an improved line of Chevrolets snatched first place in both passenger cars and trucks. Rivals Dodge and International also showed strong gains. Dodge logged retail sales of 72,501 trucks—the division had been steadily moving up the chart since 1932—while International sold over 60,000 trucks, its best year ever.

Change was in the air when it came time for Ford to introduce its 1937 trucks. That year Ford again restyled its passenger cars, and much of the new look was carried over to the sedan delivery and station wagon models. Sleek, with a flowing, slant-back grille and faired-in headlamps, the new styling was very attractive. A new car-based commercial model called the Coupe-Express (one source refers to it as the Coupe-Pickup) was introduced. It was a standard Ford coupe with a small ½-ton pickup box incorporated in the trunk area. Although prices began as low as $529, for some reason it didn't prove popular.

The balance of the 1937 ½-ton truck line also received styling updates with handsome new grille shells, a two-piece V-type windshield, and lower-mounted headlamps. There

As this 1938 advertisement says, "Two words have sold four million trucks . . . FORD ECONOMY." Ford's new styling this year was hard to ignore, with a pleasingly modern look that was simple yet stylish.

One of the best-looking light trucks of the 1930s was this 1937 Ford coupe with a pickup bed attached, introduced to compete with a similar model from Chevrolet. Rated to carry a ½-ton load, the box was 64 inches long, 33 inches wide, and 12 inches deep. These trucks were offered only for 1937.

were several important driveline changes too. The carryover V-8 was given a redesigned cylinder block with integrated, self-lubricating water pumps, new valve guides, and an improved ignition system. Base output was now listed as 85 horsepower. There was also a new economy V-8 this year. Displacing a mere 136 cubic inches, it developed 60 horsepower and became known as the V8-60. The little V-8 was offered in all commercial car models, except the station wagon, and in all 131.5-inch wheelbase trucks, except for the dump models. It proved a surprising success.

Commercial cars with the 60-horsepower V-8 were designated models 73, 74, and 75 depending on wheelbase. The 85-horsepower jobs were models 77, 78, and 79. Truck sales for the year exceeded 164,000 units.

OH GREAT, ANOTHER DEPRESSION

Then came 1938 and with it a short, sharp recession that seemed aimed especially at manufacturers. Things got so bad that the slump was termed a "mini-depression" and it halted Ford's truck sales resurgence in its tracks.

The shame of all this was that Ford offered some exceptionally fine trucks this year. Station wagons, panel trucks, and sedan deliveries all used the new front sheet metal from the passenger car line and were particularly beautiful; with large front fenders and sweptback grilles, they were practically instant classics. Heavier-duty models built on the truck chassis also got new sheet metal, but here the look was much more dramatic, with a prominent upright oval grille that was quite distinctive. The cabs were all new, with spacious interiors and generous window areas. For the first time hoods opened up from the front, alligator-style. The pickup box was all new too, as were the interior trim and instrument panel.

The 1½-ton chassis was redesigned to meet new industry standards calling for a 34-inch spacing of rear frame rails and new CA (cab to center of axle) dimensions, all enacted to bring a degree of standardization to the industry, which would help body manufacturers immeasurably. The 1½-ton jobs now got the 85-horsepower V-8 exclusively.

The 1930s were really a golden age for Ford truck styling, as can be seen in this color print of a 1937 V-8 pickup. Note the V-8 hubcaps and curved front bumper, styling details that helped make Fords so special looking.

The Ford cab-over-engine (COE) trucks for 1939 looked about the same as the 1938 models, but because the US economy was bouncing back smartly, the 1939 models sold better. At the same time, however, many Americans were feeling uneasy because war had broken out in Europe, and they worried that America might get involved. But for now, at least, the country was still at peace.

Also in 1938 new 1-ton models were introduced to span the gap between the commercial cars and the heavy-duty rigs. Built on a 122-inch wheelbase, they gave Ford dealers added firepower in a hotly contested market segment. When spring arrived, the company also debuted the interesting new cab-over-engine (COE) trucks, the first factory-produced cab-overs from Ford.

None of this did much good in the face of economic headwinds that killed sales momentum, and Ford ended up selling just over 87,000 trucks for 1938.

1939–1941

By the time 1939 rolled around, the severe downturn of 1938 had come to an end and the economy was beginning to pick up once again. But Americans, just a few years free of the Great Depression and caught by surprise in 1938 by more fiscal turmoil, were understandably uneasy, so any economic recovery was going to take time.

During 1939 war was declared in Europe, as a resurgent Germany went along with Hitler's insane plan to take over the world. The immediate effect on Ford was felt in its German plant, which was taken over by the Germans; over the war years, this plant would produce trucks for Germany's war effort. In the United Kingdom, Ford of Britain also switched over to war production, this time for the British Army and its allies. September 1939 saw Canada, as part of the British Commonwealth, also declare war on Germany, so the Ford of Canada plants were soon converted to building specially designed military trucks. Russia's GAZ factory, which built its own versions of the Ford A and AA models, now built trucks for the Russian Army.

The United States was still at peace, so Ford's plants there concentrated on civilian production. The company made a long-overdue switch over to hydraulic brakes, except on models equipped with air brakes. A larger 95-horsepower V-8, developed for Ford's new Mercury line of cars, was now optional on many Ford truck models. The carryover 85-horsepower V-8 benefited from improvements including new rings, camshaft, and crankshaft.

RIGHT: The 1939 Ford rack truck (shown here) was probably used to move freight from ships to warehouses, from which larger trucks could then be loaded for transshipment to a final destination. Ford sold more than 112,000 trucks during the year.

BELOW: A 1940 highway tractor. Ford line-haul tractors looked especially tough this year with great styling that, while shared with the smaller trucks, seemed to look better on the big rigs. Kirk Transportation actually bought several units like this. We wonder if the company is still in business after all these years.

The 1939 car-based trucks were mildly facelifted and very good-looking. The smaller truck-based models carried over their styling with only minor changes, as did the larger conventional trucks. Truck sales this year topped 112,000 units, good for second place behind Chevrolet.

But the world situation was changing. By 1940 military planners in the United States were convinced that the fighting raging in Europe and the South Pacific would eventually draw America into another war, so they took steps to prepare the country for it. Military budgets were tight because the public and Congress were against any overseas entanglements and isolationist feelings were strong in most of the country, but the army planners did everything possible. Ford was asked to take on the manufacture of aircraft engines and components to help supply Britain's urgent needs as well as those of the US Army Air Forces, so ground was broken this year on a new aircraft engine plant at the Rouge.

Ford engineers redesigned most of the company's truck chassis this year, replacing the traditional torque tube layout with a Hotchkiss drive and further standardizing

Seen here is a standard Ford express pickup riding a 122-inch wheelbase. This longbed pickup was built for bigger jobs and heavier loads than the smaller 112-inch light-duty pickup. Even the styling was different; the light pickup shared its front-end sheet metal with Ford's passenger car line while the bigger pickups looked more like the Ford heavy-duty jobs.

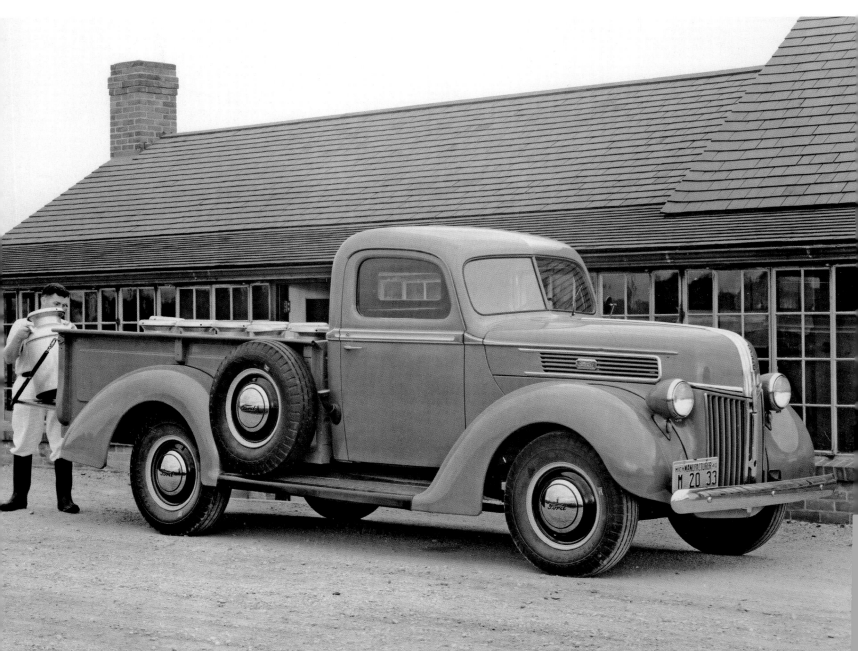

ABOVE: A 1941 Ford ½-ton pickup on a 112-inch wheelbase. As noted earlier, the light-duty pickups for 1941 used the front-end sheet metal from the passenger car line with appropriate changes. These trucks were considered part of the commercial car line that also included the sedan delivery and station wagon models.

FOLLOWING PAGES: For 1941 the Ford COE trucks finally changed their 1938-type styling to that of the other truck lines, giving them a more familial look. These tough trucks were used by thousands of companies that needed a rugged vehicle that was easy to drive in tight city spaces.

its CA dimensions to make things easier for body builders. Styling was extensively facelifted, giving the 1940 Ford medium- and heavy-duty trucks a much stronger, more forceful look. Cab-over trucks saw much less change. Sealed-beam headlamps came into popular use this year, and interestingly the ½-ton trucks adopted the look of the Ford passenger car line for the first time since 1932—as well as the last time ever. As before, Ford commercial cars utilized a modified passenger car chassis as well as outer sheet metal.

The Ford transit bus was completely redesigned and reengineered this year, switching from a front-engine to a rear-engine layout. An all-new body, provided by Union City Body Company of Union City, Indiana, looked amazingly modern and bright. Union City was a solid, high-quality supplier; years earlier they'd produced bodies for Duesenberg Motors.

Business began to turn upward as companies won orders for war materials, and new factories were being erected to fill those orders. Purchases by construction companies and delivery firms grew accordingly. Ford management could see it in the numbers: sales of Ford light trucks during 1940 grew to about 134,000 units and the company came within a whisker of outselling Chevy.

When it was time to announce the 1941 trucks, Ford Motor Company didn't have a lot to show that was new, but it did introduce a four-cylinder engine offering for the commercial car, ¾-ton, and 1-ton lines. This was the flathead four from the Ford tractor line, and it produced a mere 30 horsepower. Targeting buyers who were vitally interested in fuel economy, the new four proved popular only with light delivery companies, and even then not very. Ford COE models this year received new front styling that replaced the oval grille with one that shared a familial appearance with the medium series.

A 45-horsepower version of the Ford four-cylinder engine also made its appearance in a prototype military scout car called the GP. In a three-way shoot-out with Willys-Overland and Bantam, Ford was awarded a contract to produce some 1,500 units for the military, as were the other two, the idea being that the three designs would then be heavily tested by the military; the winner would be given the big production contract. In testing, the GP rated highly for fit, finish, and comfort but lagged the others in acceleration and off-road performance. That same year the company also won contracts for mobile field kitchen trucks and bomb service vehicles, both based on modified 1-ton civilian models.

It was destined to be a very short model run, however. On December 7, 1941, Japan launched a sneak attack on the US Navy base at Pearl Harbor, Hawaii, an act of treachery that will never be forgotten. Its effects were to heavily damage the America fleet in the Pacific—and it forced the country to declare war on Japan. The government reacted swiftly to the urgent demand for war materiel, halting automobile production in February 1942, though allowing certain companies to continue making trucks, nearly all of which were directed to the war effort.

With war declared, the gloves were off; America and its mightiest industry were committed to all-out combat, and it was going to be long, difficult, and bloody. But in the end the heroism of American soldiers combined with the production genius of American manufacturers made the result inevitable. Japan and Germany would come to rue the day they decided to take up arms against the United States.

ABOVE: The Ford stand-and-drive trucks were very popular with businesses that had route deliveries, such as bakeries and dairies. This 1941 milk truck is a perfect representative of the thousands of such units that were sold.

OPPOSITE TOP: The City Fruit & Produce Company ran a fleet of Ford trucks in the pre–World War II era. This attractive panel truck is not to be confused with the lighter-duty panel delivery, which used a similar-looking body mated to passenger-car front-end sheet metal. The heavier-duty panel truck could be ordered in ¾-ton, 1-ton, or 1½-ton versions.

OPPOSITE BOTTOM: As American industries continued to receive big orders for goods needed by countries engaged in war overseas, more workers were hired and, as a result, demand for the Ford Transit bus rose strongly. This 1941 model shows how clean and modern its lines were.

Chapter 4

THE
WAR YEARS

For most Americans the war seemed grim and confusing in early 1942. The country was still reeling from the brutal attacks on Pearl Harbor and Bataan. Next to fall would be General Douglas MacArthur's headquarters on Corregidor Island. At home, determined civilian engineers worked feverishly to convert American factories to the production of the tools of war. In this, America's auto industry would be the undisputed leader.

Ford Motor Company, as already noted, had contracts to build aircraft engines and components. Now it took on the much larger job of producing B-24 Liberator bombers in quantities that frankly seemed impossible.

The day after the ruthless bombing of Pearl Harbor, America declared war. As the nation began building up its might, the Ford Motor Company was asked to produce heavy-duty cargo trucks, such as the one shown here, for the military and for certain civilian contractors deemed vital to the war effort.

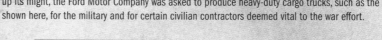

Ford also got the job of back-up supplier of the ¼-ton military GP scout car that became known as the Jeep. Willys-Overland won the prime contract based on the merits of its prototype—its powerful engine made it the best performer by far—but the army was worried that a saboteur might be able to inflict enough damage to the Willys plant to cause a halt in production of the vital scout cars, so they awarded a large contract to Ford to build Jeeps to the Willys design, right down to the engine. In truth there were a few differences between the Willys MB and the Ford GPW (General Purpose Willys), but they were minor. Ford ended up building over 277,000 units.

THE ARSENAL OF DEMOCRACY

From 1941 to 1945 Ford produced a staggering number of vehicles for the war effort in addition to the Jeeps, including thousands of armored cars, M10 tank destroyers, M20 command cars, cargo trucks, kitchen trucks, troop carriers, Sherman tanks, and an amphibian version of the Jeep known as the Seep. Ford of Canada also became a major vehicle producer for the Allied forces.

As mentioned in the previous chapter, Ford unfortunately also produced military vehicles for the Axis powers via Ford of Germany, which was taken over by the Nazis and put to work producing cars and trucks for the German Army, along with half-track vehicles.

During 1941, Ford Motor Company was one of three companies invited to produce prototypes of a new scout vehicle for the military. Ford came up with this unit, which is nicknamed the Pygmy. The other companies involved, Willys-Overland and American Bantam, produced similar vehicles. Officially called the GP, the little Ford was powered by a four-cylinder Ford tractor engine, which limited its performance compared to the powerful Willys.

That wasn't the full extent of the outrage, either; once France and Holland were overrun by German troops, the Ford plants in those countries were likewise forced to produce vehicles for the German Army.

But the Germans were unable to equal the tremendous production efficiency of the Ford plants in the free nations around the world, so although they were an aid to the Axis powers, in the end they weren't able to tip the balance of the war. Nothing on earth could match America's productive genius.

As one of the largest manufacturers in the world, Ford was looked to for a vast amount of war goods, and it delivered. Over the war years Ford produced some 57,581 aircraft engines and an incredible 8,685 B-24 bombers. The company also produced truck, tank, and Jeep engines, armor plating, aircraft generators, gun mounts, and so much more. The company even devoted part of its tremendous woodworking production capacity to produce 4,291 gliders for landing troops.

After extensive testing, the Willys-Overland scout car was chosen to be the standard Jeep. However, military planners were worried about Willys's ability to deliver the volume of vehicles needed, so they awarded a contract to Ford to also produce the Jeep, using the Willys blueprints and engine. The Ford version was called the GPW, for "General Purpose Willys." The vehicles were essentially the same, though, with a few very minor differences.

Who's in Charge

Personal tragedy struck the Ford family in May 1943 when Edsel Ford, son of the founder of Ford Motor Company, died at the age of forty-nine from stomach cancer. His loss meant that old Henry Ford, aged, cranky, and possibly becoming senile, was back in charge of the company. There seemed to be no one else who could do the job. Ford Motor was a privately owned firm and jealousy limited control to family members. Edsel was the Fords's only child, so his passing left a gap in management succession. Edsel's son, Henry Ford II (Henry's grandson), was young, inexperienced, and away serving in the US Navy. Military planners were naturally concerned about old Henry's ability to manage the vast network of production that was so vital to the war effort. The poorly managed Ford Motor Company was losing millions of dollars each month, and the US government considered taking it over to ensure the supply of military products would continue to flow out to the Allied forces. Then came a solution: After the appropriate strings were pulled, Henry Ford II was transferred out of the navy and joined the management ranks at Ford, the better to watch over the company's fortune. Although the elder Henry remained in overall control, his young grandson became a vital mover within the company.

By 1944 America's aging fleet of civilian trucks was beginning to feel the strain of being overworked; it became plain that the nation needed new trucks to replace ones that were being worn out. The government allowed a limited number to be produced for civilian purchase and Ford introduced the Model 488T chassis and cab on a 158-inch wheelbase and the Model 494T school bus chassis, both powered by the Ford V-8. Civilian customers quickly snapped them up.

VICTORY

Ford and the rest of America's manufacturing industries were crucial in turning the tide of war in the Allies's favor, and on September 2, 1945, the Empire of Japan finally surrendered, signing the formal documents aboard the USS *Missouri*. During that same year it became clear that an increasingly failing senior Henry Ford could no longer handle the responsibilities of running the company. His grandson Henry II was named president of the firm in September 1945. The young Mr. Ford was now in the hot seat of a company that was depressed, demoralized, and losing money. For the next decade he would have his hands full trying to turn the business around.

PREVIOUS PAGES: This small passenger bus, built on a 1942 Ford chassis, is fitted with a compact twelve- to fifteen-passenger bus body built by Wayne. Produced on a 134-inch wheelbase, it looks a bit stubby but apparently served a small area. This vehicle was probably built sometime in 1943 on a chassis that had been built earlier and stored until needed.

OPPOSITE: More Ford Trucks on the Road! As the ad explains, the General Baking Company operated a fleet of 3,700 Ford trucks, such as this stylish 1945 bakery delivery model. With the war over, Ford ramped up truck production to meet the needs of tens of thousands of businesses anxious for new vehicles.

MORE FORD TRUCKS ON THE ROAD !

"We know 3,700 reasons why," says General Baking Company

Delivering bread through most of the Central and Eastern half of the United States, General Baking Company operates 3,700 Ford Trucks out of their large number of big bakeries. You may be sure it wasn't anybody's whim, but strict cost-accounting, that put those sturdy, thrifty Fords to work in this great fleet. A General Baking Company official sums it up this way:

"We standardize on Ford Trucks because, first of all, the original cost is right. Second, Ford parts are easy to get. Third, the cost of maintenance is lower."

Those plain facts are the reasons why, year after year, official registrations show more Ford Trucks on the road than any other trucks in existence.

The advanced Ford Trucks being built today, in large quantities, bring you traditional Ford economy, reliability and stamina in greater measure than ever, enhanced by many important engineering advancements. Your Ford Dealer will be happy to tell you all about these added Ford Truck advantages.

FORD ADVANCED TRUCK ENGINEERING
MORE ECONOMY • MORE ENDURANCE • EASIER SERVICING

A STILL GREATER 100 HP V-8 ENGINE with NEW Ford steel-cored Silvaloy rod bearings, more enduring than ever in severe service • NEW aluminum alloy cam-ground pistons with 4 rings each, for oil economy • BIGGER, more efficient oil pump and IMPROVED rear bearing oil seal • NEW longer-lived valve springs • NEW improvements in cooling • NEW efficiency in ignition • in carburetion • in lubrication • Far-reaching advancements in ease and economy of servicing operations.

IMPORTANT FORD CHASSIS ADVANTAGES: Easy accessibility for low-cost maintenance • Universal service facilities • Heavy-duty front axle • Extra-sturdy full-floating rear axle with pinion straddle-mounted on 3 large roller bearings • 3 axle ratios available • 2-speed axle available at extra cost • Powerful hydraulic brakes, exceptionally large cast drums • Long-lived needle bearing universal joints • Rugged 4-speed transmission with NEW internal reverse lock.

FORD TRUCKS
Ford TRUCK-ENGINEERED
TRUCK-BUILT • BY TRUCK MEN

Chapter 5

YEARS OF GREATNESS

With World War II finally over, the Ford Motor Company, along with the rest of the American auto industry, was free once again to produce civilian vehicles, which were vitally needed to replace an automotive fleet that was getting old. Henry Ford II was in charge now at his grandfather's company, and he directed his team to increase civilian production as quickly as possible. First to market were trucks, which was easy enough to manage since they were fundamentally similar to the vehicles produced during the war years. On a few of the wartime models, little needed to be changed other than discontinue painting them OD (olive drab). Introduced during May, the trucks carried a 1945 model designation until November when, with little change, the 1946 model year production began. Gradually the other Ford trucks, a continuation of the prewar designs, entered production as well.

Shown here at the filling station, which is what we used to call gas stations, is a Ford F-350 stake truck. Note how the white-painted grille contrasts well with the red body paint.

By the time the 1946 model year opened, the range of truck model offerings was expanded and now included ½-, ¾-, and 1-ton pickups, vital to farmers whose rolling stock was rapidly wearing out. Wheelbase offerings included 114-inch and 122-inch lengths. These same models could be had in cab-and-chassis versions, thus permitting the installation of a variety of work bodies. Heavy-duty models offered chassis lengths of 134 inches, 158 inches, and 194 inches, the latter designed primarily for school buses. Box truck, stake truck, tanker, and school bus bodies were created to fit the needs of various end users. The long-absent panel trucks, sedan deliveries, and station wagons that would find favor with hippies and surfers in the 1960s rejoined the line this year, along with COE models and van chassis. By October 1945 Ford was producing some forty-two different truck chassis/body versions. In June 1946 the company began designating its reinforced-frame, 2-speed, rear-axle-equipped, heavy-duty models and COEs as 2-ton trucks. The company continued expanding its product range even as demand for new trucks continued to outstrip production capacity. There was only one problem in the market: civilian demand was running so far ahead of production that no company in America could hope to keep up. Thus it was critically important that no interruptions to production be allowed to occur.

For lighter jobs, such as flower and package delivery, a good choice was a ½-ton Ford panel truck such as this 1946 model. Light, easy to drive, economical, and long-lived, these trucks were purchased by pharmacies, flower shops, dry cleaning establishments, and dealers for use as service trucks.

WAR'S OVER—TIME FOR A STRIKE!

Here's an interesting unit: a 1946 Ford 1½-ton cab-over engine with dual rear wheels and fantastic styling! Note how the grille shape has a family resemblance to the light-duty Ford pickups. Cab-overs rejoined the line this year after a three-year absence.

Unfortunately, there was also a tremendous amount of labor unrest during the year as workers who had "patriotically" refrained from striking during the war years now resumed the tactic with a vengeance. Steelworkers launched a brutal strike and were followed by parts and components workers, all of which greatly depressed production and drove up costs. That was one reason why during the hottest retail environment to that point in history Ford lost another $8 million. It was due almost entirely to the strikes.

After being strikebound for much of the prior year, 1947 was sure to be better, though product-wise Ford had almost nothing that was new. However, this year was destined to be like the prior year, with pent-up demand so high that all a company had to do to sell vehicles was to produce them. Aye, as Shakespeare said, there's the rub. For just as in 1946, this year the industry struggled with labor unrest, strikes, and shortages of everything from sheet metal to taillamps. The unfortunate production planners who had to work their way through the multitude of problems affecting production schedules were to be pitied, for theirs was a thankless, difficult task.

ABOVE: Ford truck with specialized bodywork by DeKalb Commercial Body Corporation. We wish we knew what this unusual truck was used for. With its tall windshield and raised roofline, it may have been a stand-and-drive model, but for what sort of business? Any ideas?

LEFT: In addition to cab-and-chassis models, Ford offered a variety of cowl-and-chassis products as well. In this rare photo we see how the factory would piggyback two units so that one driver could deliver it. This, of course, was in the days before OSHA.

One Ford product that was enjoying high demand in 1947 was the rear-engine universal bus, Model 79D; more than 2,200 units were built during the year.

This season the advertising slogan was "Ford Trucks Last Longer" and research showed they actually did. The sturdy Fords benefited from good design and careful construction. During the year the company produced its five millionth truck. On April 7, old Henry Ford, the company's brilliant but irascible eighty-three-year-old founder, passed away quietly at Fairlane, his Michigan estate.

Control of the company had already been handed over to Ford's grandson, and by this time Henry Ford II had hired a team of ten army statistical experts, dubbed the "Whiz Kids," who were busily introducing modern management techniques to the hidebound company. The business had been poorly run the last few years of the founder's reign and there was even concern that it might go bust. But the Whiz Kids were revamping financial controls throughout Ford, and the company was starting to turn the corner after years of losses.

THE BIG BONUS OF 1948

Ford Motor Company hit the ground running for 1948, introducing a full lineup of completely revamped work-ready vehicles on January 16. This was the birth of the now-legendary Ford F-series. Dubbed the "Bonus-Built" trucks, they represented a major part of a veritable avalanche of commercial vehicles, a total of some 115 body-chassis combinations in all.

New cabs debuted with stylish sheet metal providing a much more modern appearance. Fenders were squarer than before and wrapped around the front to combine with the grille panel, which featured inset headlamps. The new cab was 65 inches wide and included a one-piece windshield, plus vent windows for driver comfort. Seats were more comfortable this year, instrument panels were redesigned, and ingress–egress was improved. The cab was mounted on insulating pads for a smoother, quieter ride. Ford now used this cab for its COE models as well as the conventional trucks. Thus, for the first time, frontal styling was similar throughout the line.

In the light-duty line, the handsome new F-1 led the way as the ½-ton line. The ¾-ton market was served by the F-2 ¾-ton and F-3 Heavy ¾-ton (formerly rated 1-ton), with the 1-ton series being designated the F-4. The F-5 and F-6 models comprised a broad line of COE and conventional work trucks.

During 1948 Ford introduced a legend: the F-series trucks. The F-1 light-duty pickup was as modern as tomorrow and as durable and well-built as anyone would expect from a Ford truck. Notice the rounded, modern lines of this truck. Who wouldn't want one today?

1948: The Legendary F-series Trucks

When Ford introduced its all-new F-1 ½-ton pickup truck for 1948, along with the heavier duty F-2 ¾-ton jobs, the company was establishing a line of trucks that quickly became legendary. The F-series trucks brought real style to the truck market with durability and capability that were second to none. Powered by a new six-cylinder engine and two new V-8s, the Fs could tackle big jobs easily and still deliver excellent fuel economy. The new cab, Ford claimed, offered "living-room comfort" and "picture-window visibility." They were, in fact, representative of a new way of thinking about trucks. From now on, comfort would become nearly as important as load-carrying capacity. Trucks were going to be more driver-friendly than ever before.

Also joining the ranks were the new 2½- and 3-ton extra heavy-duty trucks, models F-7 and F-8. They were tough: powered by an all-new V-8 engine and equipped with a stronger clutch, beefier brakes and frame, and an optional 5-speed gearbox for maximum pulling power. With the truck cab mounted on a new frame and chassis, the heaviest-duty Fords provided dealers with an ideal product to sell to customers they had never been able to before, including purchasers of cement mixers, tar spreaders, logging trucks, and the biggest coal and fuel trucks.

The new trucks, along with an improvement in the supply of raw materials and component parts, allowed Ford Motor Company to boost production for 1948 despite the best efforts of strike-happy workers to bring the industry to a screeching halt. In fact, this proved to be Ford's best year for trucks since 1929.

NO, REALLY, WE'RE GOOD

In view of the outstanding success of the all-new 1948 models, no one could fault Ford management's decision to not change very much product-wise the following year. Thus the 1949 Ford trucks were mainly carryover, though the company continued to add additional models and variations in order to appeal to as many customers as possible. By March 1949 Ford's truck line consisted of 139 models; by the end of summer, that had grown to 164 models.

There were product changes, naturally. Some were improvements, such as the addition of an item or two of standard equipment, and some were of questionable value, such as the decision to replace the F-6 and F-8 standard 2-speed rear axles with single-speed units. The F-6 models debuted a new Big Six engine. A new thirty-one- to thirty-five-passenger motorcoach riding a 182-inch wheelbase was added to the bus line.

For the year Ford managed to retail just over 165,000 trucks, down from the prior year not so much because of strikes but owing more to intense competition as the seller's market came to an abrupt end.

FOLLOWING PAGES: The most iconic of all ice cream trucks in history are the famous Good Humor trucks of the 1950s and 1960s. Thousands of these special-bodied Ford trucks hit the road each summer. The sound of their bell was one of the most exciting things for any child to hear.

1950

The 1950 model year was one of further improvements and revisions to the F-series, aimed at producing a better truck for the customer. By this point the total number of Ford models was around 175 and the company's dealers were able to supply just about any need in the marketplace. Styling was little changed and no one really expected to see much of an increase in sales, if any. However, the unique situation in the world created a big jump in demand for vehicles and Ford sales soared to over a quarter of a million trucks during the year. The reason? Fighting had broken out on the Korean Peninsula, where hoards of North Korean troops were flowing into South Korea with the self-proclaimed goal of "liberating" that sovereign nation. The armed forces of South Korea were thrown back initially, until reinforced by American troops.

All of this had an effect on the home front, where the public became concerned that car production would once again be halted for a war—as it was from 1942 to 1945. That fear drove demand to new heights as anxious car and truck buyers flocked to Ford showrooms.

OPPOSITE: Big jobs call for a rugged truck, and here we see a 1950 Ford F-7 dump truck at work. With a heavy-duty chassis, heavy-duty wheels (duals at the rear), and a beefy frame, these trucks were built for rough use.

BELOW: Tough and pretty is a good way to describe this 1950 Ford F-5. Appearance changes from earlier models was minor. Notice the optional roof-mounted cab lights.

1951–1952

Demand for new trucks eventually cooled off so that 1951 model year sales, while still very strong, were lower than the prior year. Part of this came as a result of government restrictions on raw materials, which affected production. Chrome, zinc, and copper were all in short supply, and whitewall tires were extremely hard to come by.

It would have been a different story had normal market conditions existed because the 1951 Ford trucks benefited from great new styling. Changes included a bold, aggressive new grille that spanned the full width of the front, incorporating stylish headlight nacelles into the center grille bar theme. Hood fronts were redesigned. The nicely updated Five-Star Cab featured a rear window that was 50 percent larger, as well as dual windshield wipers and an updated instrument panel. New bumpers debuted on the F-1, F-2, and F-3 models. Ford parcel delivery vans, buses, and cab-over models each were given a new look via redesigned grilles that shared a family look with the rest of the Ford truck lines. In all, Ford managed to sell over 191,000 trucks during the year.

For 1952 a new overhead-valve six-cylinder engine, dubbed the Cost Clipper Six, was available in the F-1 through F-5 models as well as parcel delivery vans. Displacing 215 cubic inches, this new engine produced 101 horsepower. Also debuting were new 279-cid and 317-cid "Cargo King" overhead-valve V-8s, the latter developing 155 horsepower. These were initially reserved for the F-7 and F-8 models; the lighter jobs continued to use the venerable flathead V-8.

This year Ford introduced a stylish new commercial car based on the Ford passenger station wagon. The Courier was a two-door Ranch Wagon with closed rear quarters instead of windows. Providing 102 cubic feet of carrying space, it included a side-hinged rear door for easy access.

But 1952 was a year of highs and lows. On the one hand, Ford Motor Company produced its thirty-nine millionth vehicle that year, a notable accomplishment. On the other hand, production and sales of its truck lines sank, with just under 125,000 trucks retailed for the year. The problem was once again the Korean War; the federal government had clamped restrictions on the number of vehicles a manufacturer could produce, and that alone killed any hope of having a good year. In addition, raw materials were in short supply and competition from Chevrolet, Dodge, Studebaker, and International was intense. In the face of all this pressure, Ford's share of the truck market fell to a postwar low. With the company's fiftieth anniversary just around the corner, however, Henry Ford II was determined to reverse the downward trend of Ford sales and make the 1953 model year one of historic proportions.

The biggest Fords were reserved for the biggest jobs, such as this Ford tractor pulling a cattle trailer. This 1950 model was one of about 175 distinct models the company fielded that year.

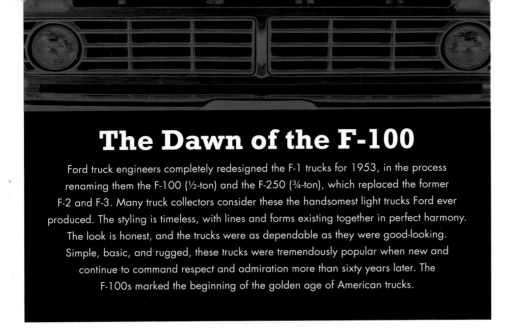

The Dawn of the F-100

Ford truck engineers completely redesigned the F-1 trucks for 1953, in the process renaming them the F-100 (½-ton) and the F-250 (¾-ton), which replaced the former F-2 and F-3. Many truck collectors consider these the handsomest light trucks Ford ever produced. The styling is timeless, with lines and forms existing together in perfect harmony. The look is honest, and the trucks were as dependable as they were good-looking. Simple, basic, and rugged, these trucks were tremendously popular when new and continue to command respect and admiration more than sixty years later. The F-100s marked the beginning of the golden age of American trucks.

1953: TIME FOR A COOL CHANGE

Pudgy, stubborn, young Henry Ford II went into the company's anniversary year backed by a $30 million styling and engineering program to bring about the sales increase he wanted. The new product program resulted in a line of completely redesigned trucks. A new "driverized" cab boasted a larger curved windshield and a 4-foot-wide rear window for greater visibility, larger side windows for a bright, airy-feeling interior, a wider seat with no-sag springs, and a stylishly curved wraparound instrument panel. New hood louvers provided an air inlet for the optional fresh-air heater.

The new styling was lower, sleeker, and more purposeful-looking than before and these models rank among the best-looking trucks Ford ever produced.

Dubbed the Ford Economy Trucks, the 1953 line introduced a revision in model nomenclature. The F-series name continued on Ford conventional trucks, but other models now had their own series designations. School bus chassis were now dubbed the B-series, COE models (now termed "forward cab") were the C-series, and parcel delivery trucks were the P-series, all of which made it much easier for customers to understand.

The F-series trucks used a longer numerical designation this year, with the ½-ton F-1 now referred to as the F-100. The F-2 and F-3 were combined into one ¾-ton model dubbed the F-250. The F-4 became the 1-ton F-350. Trucks got a new setback front axle that provided easier steering and a reduced turning diameter. For the first time ever, Ford F-100s could be ordered with an optional automatic transmission.

Ford entered the extra heavy-duty market this year with the new F-900, which had a GVWR of 27,000 pounds. Powered by the 155-horsepower Ford V-8 driven through a 5-speed gearbox, the F-900 had a GCWR of 55,000 pounds.

Henry Ford II's efforts to increase sales worked like a charm with the company reporting retail sales in 1953 of more than 200,000 trucks. Ford car sales likewise shot up as the company enjoyed one of its best years ever.

NO MORE FLATHEADS, DADDY-O!

For 1954 Ford management elected to drop the hoary old flathead V-8, replacing it with a line of more powerful and modern Y-block overhead-valve V-8s. The base Y-block was about the same displacement as the flathead but produced 15 percent more power while delivering slightly better fuel economy. In other engine news the "Mileage Maker Six" was updated and now produced 115 horsepower.

Also in 1954 the heavy-duty line could be ordered with tandem rear axles for extra hauling ability. Trucks set up with the tandem axles were designated the T-700 and T-800 models. Two new COE models, the C-700 and C-900, also debuted. The basic Ford Courier delivery car benefited from some minor styling updates, including ribbed bumpers and a sharp new grille. The F-series and C-series models also got new grilles and other minor changes.

In the insanely competitive 1954 market, Ford was able to keep up the pressure on dealers to move the metal, and sales came in almost as high as the prior year, falling less than four thousand units.

Despite a lack of substantial changes to the 1955 truck line, Henry Ford II exhorted his dealers to sell ever-higher numbers of cars and trucks. In this regard he had the

The 1955 Ford F-100, like all F-series trucks this year, received a new "drop center" grille, hood badge, and parking lamps, along with a few minor mechanical improvements. This model year ended up being a record year for the automotive industry.

weight of history on his side because 1955 was destined to be the greatest year in the history of the auto industry up to that point. The world was at relative peace, the economy was strong, restrictions on materials and production were lifted, and automakers introduced many new—and now legendary—models. It was a great time to be alive and in the market for a new car or truck.

What Ford didn't have going this year was a lot of newness to attract buyers. There were, however, some important improvements. The Ford truck line for 1955 included a restyled Courier featuring a wraparound windshield, flatter hood line, and stylish new grille, while the F-series and heavy-duty trucks received new "drop center" grilles, new hood badges and parking lamps, and assorted mechanical improvements. Despite the lack of anything really exciting to lure the public, Ford trucks sales inched upward for 1955 and the company reportedly attained its highest market penetration ever, some 30 percent.

1956: SAFETY? WHO NEEDS THAT?

After such an exciting, record-setting year as 1955, it was natural to suppose that 1956 would see an easing in demand for new cars and trucks, and that's exactly what happened. Ford Motor Company was in decent shape product-wise for 1956, debuting new safety features in a company-wide drive to improve survivability in accidents while reducing injuries as well. A new interlocking door latch design that helped keep doors shut in an accident was introduced on trucks after tests proved it kept passengers safer by keeping them inside the vehicle during a crash. Also debuting was a new deep-dish steering wheel that reduced incidents of chest injuries in collisions. Both of these features were eventually adopted by the industry as a whole, but in 1956 they didn't stir much interest. The joke back then was that "Ford sold safety while Chevrolet sold cars," and unfortunately it was true.

Style-wise the conventional trucks received new grilles and wraparound windshields, and the net result of these two changes was quite handsome; the windshield in particular greatly updated the cab's appearance. To meet customer demands for more power, the V-8 engines were increased in displacement and power, and four-barrel carburetors were now

The 1956 Ford F-100, shown here with a contrasting roof color, shows how stylish and desirable these trucks really were. Considering the amount of utility they offered at a very reasonable price, it's no wonder they were so popular.

Here's a good look at the interior of a 1956 Ford F-100 pickup. The interior, while rather plain, features durable seats with good-quality upholstery and well-finished door panels. The floor covering is a black rubber mat for easy cleanup.

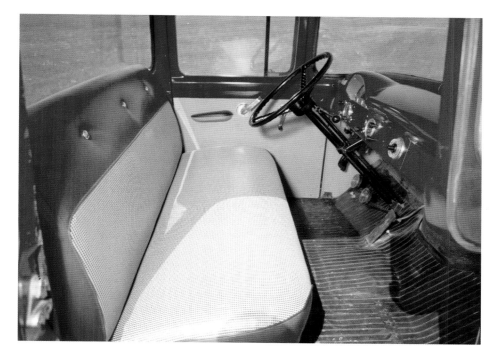

available as well. The ¾-ton and larger models offered tubeless tires that were becoming popular, and a new T-750 tandem model debuted. The number of truck models now stood at an amazing 289.

In January Ford Motor Company went public, having been a privately owned business since its early days. Old Henry probably turned in his grave over his family's decision to finally sell stock to the public—he always detested the interference of partners and shareholders—but in the end it was the right thing to do. The Ford Motor Company needed money to expand the business, and going public would bring in tons of fresh capital. In point of fact, that same year the company announced it was launching a $530 million expansion program.

In another tradition-breaking move, Ford joined the Automobile Manufacturers Association, headed just then by George Romney of American Motors, who'd used his considerable salesmanship to help convince Henry Ford II to make the move. Meanwhile Ford truck sales fell to 184,000 during 1956, but the company was tooling up an all-new line for introduction in the fall, so 1957 was almost certain to be a better year.

1957: ALL NEW AND BEAUTIFUL TOO

The 1957 Ford trucks were completely new and sharply different from prior years. Cabs were wider and boldly styled, with straight-through fenders, concealed running boards, huge wraparound windshields, and a full-width hood that capped the fenders as well as the engine bay. On pickup models a new full-width bed was offered at a slight premium over the more traditional style with separate rear fenders. The new look was clean, modern, and big.

Betting the Ranchero

Ford caught the entire US truck industry off-guard when it introduced the new Ranchero "pickup car." Based on the good-looking Ford passenger car line, the Ranchero was a "gentleman's pickup" because it offered great styling and available trim that could really dude it up. With bold two-tone paint jobs and whitewall tires, the Ranchero could be every bit as fancy as a Lincoln—well, almost—and still haul bales of hay and bags of grain like any other truck. And it had the market all to itself, at least for a while.

Because Ford also restyled its car lines this year, the company was able to field a new car-based light-duty pickup truck called the Ranchero, and it was a surprise hit. Available in standard and custom models, no other company had anything like Ford's stylish new half-car, half-truck hybrid. Caught napping, Chevrolet truck designers immediately went to work developing a competitor for the stylish new contender.

The Ford C-series COE trucks were also completely redesigned for 1957 with handsome, squared-off styling and a cab that could be tilted forward for ease of servicing the engine. The design was so right, so nearly perfect, it would remain in production for more than two decades.

Although Ford outsold Chevy in passenger cars for 1957, it was unable to top its rival in truck sales, despite its stylish new vehicles. It did manage, however, to retail over 213,000 units for the year, and that was a substantial increase over 1956.

1958: LET'S FORGET THIS YEAR EVER HAPPENED

Considering the momentum Ford had in the marketplace, a reasonable person would have expected a further increase for 1958, but alas it was not meant to be. A major downturn in the economy, dubbed the Eisenhower Recession, knocked the pins out from under the automotive industry. It was a bad year all around for everyone (except American Motors, where Rambler sales were soaring). How bad was it? Total industry sales fell by more than 1.4 million units, Ford truck sales fell by more 64,000 units, and the company introduced the Edsel passenger car, which immediately bombed. In other words, a really bad year.

However, in some areas it actually was a good year for Ford: the company introduced new Super Duty models designed to compete in the heaviest rated segments. Single-axle Super Duty trucks could be ordered with GVWRs of 36,000 pounds and the tandem-axle jobs could have GVWRs as high as 51,000 pounds. Some of the heaviest models came with air brakes as standard equipment and all of them had beefy frames, axles, and suspensions. They were powered by new Super Duty V-8s, developed from the ground up as truck engines rather than adapted from car powerplants.

There was an industry-wide move to quad headlamps for 1958, and Ford went along with the crowd, installing four lamps on all its truck lines except for the P-series delivery

PREVIOUS PAGES: Judging by this photo, it appears that a group of Ford engineers had a little too much time on their hands and decided to see what would happen if they flew an F-100 off a ramp. We'll bet it held up just fine. Note the line of stylish Ford trucks in the background.

ABOVE: One of the most exciting Ford trucks of all time was the new Ranchero introduced for 1957. Combining the looks and style of a modern passenger car with the carrying ability of a light truck, the Ranchero was a smooth-riding, quiet truck for a gentleman farmer or a family man who occasionally needed to haul things.

trucks. The Ranchero and Courier models shared the styling updates seen on Ford's passenger cars, so they were especially stylish this year.

For the final year of the decade, Ford product planners managed to put through a number of fairly significant styling updates to the Ford line of conventional trucks, and the net effect was quite appealing. There was a very attractive new grille on conventional cab models from the F-100 on up.

This year Ford also offered its first factory-catalogued four-wheel-drive trucks, in pickup and chassis-cab versions for both the F-100 and F-250 models. Prior to this, four-wheel-drive conversions had been made on Ford trucks by several firms, most prominent of

LEFT: This is the Ford F-250 Custom Cab pickup for 1959. Although the truck was spec'd with a chrome front bumper and two-tone paint, the buyer apparently didn't feel any need for hubcaps or a rear bumper. Regardless, it's a good-looking work truck.

BELOW: Sporting dual rear wheels and a dump body, this 1959 F-800 was built for hard work. These trucks could be ordered with a variety of heavy-duty options, including air brakes or a 4-speed auxiliary transmission.

One of the most popular Ford trucks of all time is the C-series, which were used by tens of thousands of moving companies and delivery companies. Sears, Roebuck and Company ran a big fleet of these delivery trucks for many years. Shown here is a 1959 model.

which was Marmon-Herrington. Now, however, buyers could purchase a factory-produced four-wheel-drive Ford truck, and at a more reasonable price too. The new four-wheel-drive Fords proved popular as wreckers, snowplows, and construction company vehicles.

Ford's truck range now included a bewildering 370 models. At the top of the F-series were the F-1000 and F-1100 Super Duty trucks, equipped with powerful V-8 engines and available with tractor packages for hauling trailers.

The Ford Courier became a lot less "truckish" this year with the adoption of a conventional station wagon tailgate and transom rather than the side-opening cargo door used previously. Couriers also came exclusively with side window glass now rather than closed quarters, so unless one got up close enough to notice the lack of rear seats, it could easily be mistaken for the Ranch Wagon passenger car. In a similar vein, the Ranchero now offered only a Custom model, as light-truck buyers were indicating they wanted more luxury in their utility vehicles.

Ford Motors Company dealers retailed more than 210,000 light trucks for 1959. It was a good year, but the best was yet to come. During the coming decade Ford would aggressively push to try to become America's number one truck company.

Chapter 6

FORD EXPANDS THE LINE

DOWN ON THE RANCHERO

The dawn of a new decade is nearly always an exciting time; there is so much to look forward to, so many possibilities. For 1960 this was especially true as the Ford Motor Company fielded an amazing 488 different truck variations in an effort to build more volume. Ford wasn't alone in this: rivals Chevrolet, Dodge, and International each offered a plethora of competitive models. Even Studebaker, Willys, Diamond T, White, and REO were still in there taking small bites of the market.

This 1962 Ford H-series COE diesel-powered tractor was most at home on the highway where its brawny power and long-legged gearing could move the heaviest loads smoothly and competently. Cab-over models were very popular at the time because of regulations that limited the length of tractor-trailer combinations. Since a cab-over was shorter in length than a conventional tractor, it could haul a longer trailer, producing more income for the driver.

Ford claimed its new trucks offered "Certified Economy, Certified Durability and Certified Reliability" this year, and truth be told they were extremely good vehicles. Two-barrel carburetors were introduced on some models to offer a better balance between fuel economy and power. The big dogs, the F-1100 and C-1100, became 36,000-pound GVWR straight jobs only and were considered off-road trucks.

At the other end of the scale, the Ranchero was redesigned this year on the new Ford Falcon chassis and thus became a compact truck. Rated to carry an 800-pound payload, the light-duty Ranchero was aimed at what appeared to be an emerging small truck market and offered up to 30 miles per gallon from its new overhead-valve, 144-cubic-inch, six-cylinder engine.

In between these two extremes were the bread-and-butter trucks, the F-series pickups, panels, stakes, dumps, and more. The handsome Ford commercials were now in the fourth year of their design cycle but holding up well style-wise. The F-100 through F-600 models got a new lower grille and twin-vent hood front that helped freshen the front end while an expanded range of engine options enhanced the appeal of the larger truck models. Styling of the F-700 and larger trucks was carried over essentially unchanged, though these models did benefit from numerous mechanical improvements to reliability and capability. Cab-over models likewise looked about the same as before but offered higher GVWRs this year.

Although Ford offered nearly five hundred distinct variations of trucks for 1960, the F-100 was its bread-and-butter model. And is it any wonder? The bold, rugged styling and solid engineering were a strong attraction. The two-tone paint on this Custom Cab model is especially striking.

Sharing the same basic cab and styling with the plebian F-100 was the big 1960 F-600 model, shown here with a sturdy dump body. Notice the extra-large wheels fitted to ensure sufficient strength for even the heaviest loads. The combination of a bright grille with a painted front bumper looks a little odd, but it's a work truck, not a show horse after all.

The Ford Courier sedan delivery now boasted styling updates in line with those seen on the 1960 Ford passenger cars and were great-looking vehicles. The 1960 Ford four-wheel-drive models were given heavier-duty clutches and springs to enhance their already-impressive durability. Ford light-truck sales for 1960 were a reported 208,895 units.

LAST CALL!

For what would prove to be its final curtain call, the conventional Ford panel truck produced on an F-series chassis was unveiled with only routine updates. Ford had an all-new type of product undergoing final testing that would soon render the venerable panel trucks obsolete.

During the year a specially designed military vehicle went into volume production. Dubbed the M151 MUTT (Military Utility Tactical Truck), it was engineered to replace the military Jeep MD in the army's fleet, and Ford had been developing it since around 1951.

1961

Then came the 1961 model year, one of the most exciting ever. Ford Motor Company went all-out to capture new business, entering two market segments it hadn't been in before and significantly revamping the F-series, T-series, and B-series trucks. All of this represented a major investment in the truck business for Ford, a sort of gauntlet thrown down to its competitors.

As in the prior year, the lower end of the Ford truck line was anchored by the diminutive Falcon-based Ranchero and sedan delivery trucks featuring new grilles and an optional 170-cid inline six-cylinder engine good for 101 horsepower.

Next up the scale were the all-new Ford Econoline E-series trucks. These boxy vans on a compact 90-inch wheelbase were highly efficient in their use of space and were brought out partly in response to the popularity of the imported VW vans. The unibody Econoline offered a complete range of models including panel-type delivery vans with and without side windows, pickup models, school bus models, and station buses, which were window vans

Here we see three 1961 light-duty Ford truck models. Left to right they are an F-100 Custom Cab pickup with fancy two-tone paint, an Econoline pickup, also two-toned, and a green Ranchero pickup. Ford this year was pushing for a greater share of the truck market.

with seating for up to eight passengers. Ford wasn't alone in wanting to compete in this new market segment; Chevrolet was introducing its new Corvair-based van this same year.

Ford's well-loved F-series trucks came in for a complete revamping this year. The F-100 through F-700 models featured new cabs, longer wheelbases, and front-end sheet metal with reduced overhang, while the F-750 and larger trucks took on the styling of the 1960 light-duty trucks. Even more exciting was the integrated Styleside pickup box that eliminated the break in sheet metal between the cab and the box. The F-100 through F-700 trucks also got new dropped frames to reduce step-in height.

There was a new H-series of Ford trucks: large heavy-duty line-haul tractors with tilt cabs and a choice of Ford Super Duty gas engines or Cummins diesel engines, the latter a first-time offering by Ford. A choice of tough Spicer or Fuller transmissions was available as well.

The P-series delivery trucks and C-series cab-overs were mostly carryover this year, though with minor styling updates.

The industry trade paper *Automotive News* reported that Ford retailed 224,925 light trucks for 1961.

1962: WHAT'S IN A NAME?

When the new model year opened, shoppers learned that Ford management had decided to rename the station wagon version of the Econoline van. For 1962 it was called the Falcon Station Bus (some sources refer to it as the Falcon Econoline Station Bus). Standard equipment was upgraded. The other Econoline models now offered heavier GVWRs and the 170-cid inline six as options.

Falcon Ranchero and sedan delivery models received some styling updates—a new hood, grille, and front bumper, along with new taillamps.

Buyer resistance to the F-series integrated Styleside pickup box introduced the year before forced Ford to reintroduce the separate box style as seen on the earlier 1957 through 1960 trucks. Exactly what the problem was is difficult to learn at this distance, but worries about body flex causing rippled sheet metal were a likely concern. This year the more modern Cruise-O-Matic transmission replaced the older Fordomatic on F-100s.

For 1962 the F-750 model was given the frontal appearance of the lesser F-series trucks and now mated the medium-duty truck frame and suspension with the 800-series 332 HD engine. The F-100 through F-600 trucks were mainly carryover with minor appearance changes.

According to published sources, Ford dealers retailed over 260,000 light trucks during 1962.

In 1962 the passenger version of the Econoline van was called the Ford Falcon Club Wagon and came with five windows on each side, better interior trim than the work van, and a choice of seating options. Exterior trim was also fancier, in keeping with its family appeal.

1963

It was another good year for Ford trucks. The 1963 F-series light trucks received an especially handsome grille consisting of six rows of floating rectangles, which endowed the vehicles with a front-end appearance that was modern and attractive. This was the last year for the Styleside integrated beds; as sharp-looking as always, they simply failed to catch on with buyers.

Deciding to become a bigger player in the heavy-truck field this year, the company introduced the all-new N-series short conventional trucks. Designed to provide a lower-cost alternative to the big tilt-cab jobs, the N-series utilized a conventional cab layout with the F-series cab mated to new front-end sheet metal. The new N-series offered a choice of Ford gasoline engines or Cummins diesels and offered GCWRs of up to 76,800 pounds.

Other new diesel models included the Ford F-960-D, F-1000-D, F-1100-D, T-850-D, and T-950-D, which were powered by the reliable and economical Cummins V-6 diesel. Ford P-series delivery chassis also offered a diesel option.

For some reason the fancy Styleside pickups never really caught on with the buying public so 1963 would be the final year for them. It was too bad—just look how handsome and sleek this F-100 Custom Cab looks compared to an ordinary bed truck. The "spear" side molding adds a nice touch.

What's Happening?

By 1964 it was apparent to most people in the auto industry that something new was occurring within the truck market. The volume of business was growing, and what was striking about this was that many of the buyers were people who ordinarily purchased cars, not trucks. They were suburban men who wanted a truck as a second vehicle, one that could pick up supplies at the hardware store, or haul gravel for a new walkway, or take stuff to the dump. Hunters were buying four-wheel-drive pickups to haul campers for trips into the woods, and moms were buying station buses and sport utility vehicles for hauling scout troops around suburbia. These new buyers were becoming a powerful force in the market; in fact, by year-end more than a million trucks had been retailed in the United States, a new record.

These newbies to the truck field were demanding more from manufacturers. They wanted fancier interior trim, more style on the exterior, and more power under the hood. Many were interested in luxury touches such as premium radios, power steering and brakes, power windows, and air conditioning. At Ford, product planners worked to bring new options and models to market as quickly as possible.

LEFT: Four-wheel-drive pickups were gaining in favor in the early 1960s, especially with hunters, outdoorsmen, and those working in the construction trades. This 1963 F-250 4x4 would have made an ideal work/family truck for most buyers. Note the high stance and ample ground clearance.

BELOW: Another good-looking Ford pickup that never really caught on with buyers was the Econoline pickup, as seen here. This 1963 model wears the popular two-tone paint treatment that really dresses up the look.

Ford dealers had a record year in 1963, delivering a whopping 304,364 light trucks to buyers in the United States. Anyone might have expected this to be the high point for a few years, but instead it marked just another steppingstone in the growth of the US truck market. That market was growing by leaps and bounds, with no end in sight.

1964

Product changes in the Ford truck line for 1964 included a new cargo box for F-100 and F-250 two-wheel-drive pickups that featured two significant improvements: double-wall construction and the industry's first single-handle tailgate latch. The F-100 and F-250 also got a new 128-inch wheelbase for the long-bed versions.

A new budget-priced Econoline model debuting was a stripped panel van. It lacked side cargo doors and was now the least-expensive E-series model.

In the heavy-duty lines, several new Cummins economy diesel engines were introduced to replace existing engine options. The V6E-195 replaced the V6-200, the V8E-235 replaced the old V8-265, and the NHE225 replaced the former NH250, all with the aim of increased fuel economy.

Ford was feeling a capacity pinch this year so it transferred light-duty F-series production from Lorain, Ohio, where it shared production space with the Econoline series, to its Wayne Assembly Plant, which previously built cars. Renamed the Michigan Truck Plant, it would be able to focus more attention on building the popular F-series. For the year, Ford sold over 324,000 light trucks, a new record and its third such success in a row.

1965: RIDE LIKE A DREAM ON TWIN I-BEAM

There was big product news in the ½-ton and ¾-ton Ford trucks this year with the introduction of completely revamped chassis and modest styling updates. A major innovation was the new twin I-beam front suspension that was now standard on two-wheel-drive F-100 and F-250 models. It provided noticeable improvements to ride and handling along with tremendous durability. These trucks and the F-350 also offered new engine choices: heavy-duty 240-cid and 300-cid sixes and the mighty 352-cid V-8.

This year the big N-600 through N-750 models added a 199-inch wheelbase chassis while the Econoline series added extended versions with 18-inch-longer bodies. Falcon Ranchero offered optional Futura sport trim to dress things up on the exterior. But for its stablemate, the sedan delivery, this would be the final year of production. Not offered this year were the 201-inch CT tandem trucks and the P-series chassis-cab models.

This proved to be a record-breaking year for the American auto industry with over ten million vehicles sold. Of that total, Ford sold just under two million cars along with more than 389,000 trucks—a fantastic effort, but the company had momentum and it looked like it might just beat that record in 1966.

ABOVE: This 1965 heavy-duty F-950 is set up as a single-axle dual rear wheel tractor hauling what appears to be a trailer built for liquids. During the calendar year, Ford sold more than 389,000 trucks in the United States and many more in overseas markets.

LEFT: Seen here on the final assembly line is a 1965 F-series pickup with the Stepside bed. Though considered old-fashioned by some, the Stepside bed had many fans among traditionalists who appreciated the ease of getting into the bed from the side. This year the company introduced revamped chassis featuring a new twin I-beam front suspension, standard on two-wheel-drive F-100 and F-250 models. It provided improvements to ride, handling, and durability.

1966: WATCH OUT, SCOUT!

The four-wheel-drive market was experiencing strong growth in America, and Ford was taking a good chunk of the four-wheel-drive pickup segment. One niche, however, had been owned by Kaiser Jeep (formerly Willys Motors) since 1945 and that was the compact sport utility market. The Jeep CJ-5 and CJ-6 were America's favorite small sport utility vehicles, followed by the Jeep Wagoneer and Jeep's only real domestic competitor, the International Scout, introduced for 1961. Overnight the Scout had become International's best-selling vehicle, which no doubt caught the eye of Ford management. They authorized development of a small Ford competitive vehicle that would debut this year. Called the Bronco, it was a lot more like the Scout than the Jeep CJ. Riding a short 92-inch wheelbase, Broncos were offered in three body styles: roadster, wagon, or pickup. Power was supplied by Ford's reliable 170-cid six, with the 289-cid V-8 becoming available a few months later. Bronco also offered a folding windshield, 2-speed transfer case, and a choice of removable tops. Aimed at the heart of the SUV market, the Bronco was an immediate hit.

The Ranchero was back this year wearing crisp all-new sheet metal that was shared with the redesigned Falcon line. Offered in standard and Custom trim, the Ranchero rode a 113-inch wheelbase and could be ordered with payload capacity of up to 1,250 pounds. F-series trucks this year were mainly carryover as the company focused on its other truck lines, though the F-100 4x4 models got a new monobeam front axle that provided a significantly lower ride height while maintaining good ground clearance.

The aging heavy-duty H-series trucks were replaced midyear by the new W-series cab-overs, which offered diesel power exclusively and were quite distinctive-looking, with flat-face styling that was clean and modern. The Ws offered a broad range of diesel options that included Cummins, Detroit Diesel, and Caterpillar engines. The line featured a BBC dimension of just 52 inches without a sleeper, and a choice of single or tandem rear axles.

ABOVE: This neat truck is one that would be hard to find today: a 1965 F-250 crew-cab pickup. The crew-cab designation meant it had four doors, for hauling work crews; construction companies or firms that worked in off-road areas usually purchased these models.

OPPOSITE TOP: Rarely seen today is the 1966 Bronco pickup, which is a shame because they are a delightful vehicle to own and drive. Note the freewheeling hubs installed on the front wheels; they helped reduce front-end wear and improve fuel economy.

OPPOSITE BOTTOM: At first glance this appears to be a bone stock 1966 F-100 with two-tone paint, but closer examination reveals it's a 4x4 model—note the freewheeling hubs on the front wheels and the slightly taller-than-normal ride height. The new twin I-beam suspension helped to lower the truck's silhouette. This vehicle is also equipped with trailer mirrors and optional fender-mounted indicator lights, so it's probably safe to assume it was spec'd to carry a slide-in camper. If it had been planned as a tow vehicle, the buyer would more than likely have specified an F-250.

Indicating a shift in market preferences this year, car sales were down on an industry-wide basis while light-duty truck sales were up. Ford sold just under 430,000 light trucks for the year. Chevy did over half a million, so despite Ford's best effort they were still not the number one seller in the US market.

1967: THE GOLDILOCKS RANCHERO

Compact cars were once a hot segment in the market and compact trucks had their turn in the limelight too, but the market was turning toward larger units now. The feeling at Ford seems to have been that the original Ranchero was too big, the Falcon Ranchero too small, so a midsize Ranchero would, as Goldilocks might have said, be "just right." Thus for 1967 the Ford Ranchero was redesigned on the larger Fairlane body. Goldilocks was right; it was a great-looking truck.

There were many changes to the F-series trucks this year. A wider cab debuted with improved seating and shoulder room, along with better visibility via larger curved-glass side windows, plus improved ventilation. Appearance differences between the light-duty

The 1967 W-1000 cab-over featured a wide cab for comfort, though it was quite short in overall length, the better to haul longer trailers. Pride of ownership had come to the big rigs, and many were ordered with stylish two-tone paint schemes like the one shown. Although it was a down year for truck sales, Ford still sold more than four hundred thousand light trucks in the United States.

F-100 through F-350 range and the medium-duty F-500 through F-750 models were more extensive than before. The bigger trucks got their own front-end sheet metal this year that gave them a larger, more rugged look despite the shared cabs.

The Bronco, now in its second year, offered new Sport trim for the pickup and station wagon models. In addition, all Broncos received upgraded standard equipment with the addition of self-adjusting brakes, padded sun visors, back-up lights, dual master cylinders, and more. Bronco's popularity continued to increase.

The heaviest Ford trucks offered new diesel engines built by British firm Dorset, along with several new Detroit Diesel options.

Some years earlier, Ford had somehow lost the bidding to produce the M151 MUTT military scout cars—Willys Motors snatched the contract—but Ford won it back, and this year was awarded a new contract to produce quantities for the US Army.

After having enjoyed a string of sales increases, the truck market slowed down just a bit this year. Ford sales slipped to 411,000 units, a tremendous year regardless.

1968

Ford Ranchero got a facelift this year, with horizontal quad headlamps replacing the stacked quads seen in the prior year. Smoother lines and a longer, sleeker profile endowed it with the appearance of an all-new vehicle.

Ford Econoline and Club Wagon were all new for 1968, with larger, longer bodies boasting short front hoods for easier routine engine servicing. Two wheelbase lengths were offered, and a 302-cid V-8 engine was now available. The front suspension now featured Ford's famous twin I-beams for a lower ride height and greater durability.

The Bronco returned with minor changes that included revised bumpers, side-marker lights, and improved interior fittings. All models now offered freewheeling front hubs to reduce front end wear as well as to improve fuel economy.

This year saw Ford continue to revamp its truck lines with an all-new Econoline that was more capable than ever. Three models were offered: the base E-100 with a 4,500-pound GVWR, an E-200 with a 5,400-pound GVWR, and the rugged E-300 with a 7,600-pound GVWR. There were two wheelbases available: 105.5 inches and 123.5 inches. In the redesign the engine was pushed forward under a short hood in order to make it easier to service while reducing interior intrusion and providing more frontal impact protection. Econolines now featured twin I-beam front suspension and were offered with an optional 302-cid V-8. To simplify the lineup, the slow-selling Econoline pickup was dropped. The family station wagon model was now known as the Club Wagon, and a school bus package was again offered.

In the conventional light-duty truck line, new 360-cid and 390-cid V-8s became available, while the heavier F-series trucks and B-series school bus chassis now offered the Dorset diesel engine as an option.

The big jobs, the Ford W-series trucks, were essentially carryover this year but with a handful of new safety features, such as side-marker lights and reflectors.

Ford light trucks proved amazingly popular again this year as sales blew well past the half million mark.

1969

Consumers were demanding more power and comfort in sport utility vehicles so the Bronco was given the 302-cid engine as a new base V-8, though the wimpy 170-cid six continued as standard equipment for six-cylinder versions. F-100s also got the 302-cid V-8 while Rancheros got a big new 250-cid straight six as standard equipment along with a 351-cid V-8 option, just the thing to order with the popular Ranchero GT trim.

Several less popular models were culled from the ranks, including the F-250 chassis-cab unit, the base Bronco roadster, and the F-100 6.5-foot-long stake truck.

The medium and heavy C-series trucks were still in the lineup, looking about the same because their styling was seemingly ageless and difficult to improve upon. The same

ABOVE: "A cab-over with a reefer on" is how a truck driver would describe this outfit. It's a 1970 C-series tilt-cab straight job, meaning it's on a full frame rather than set up as a tractor towing a trailer. "Reefer" refers to the refrigerated box used for hauling perishable food. These trucks were often used by in-city fleets for delivering food to grocery stores and supermarkets.

LEFT: A big L-series truck cruises down the road hauling a trailer load of—who knows? The unit is operated by Associated Transport Company. The tractor is a 1971 model with tandem rear axles. Sources claim Ford offered more than one thousand truck model variations this year.

could be said of the W-series trucks; these sturdy haulers just seemed to go on and on.

Ford entered the motorhome chassis market in a big way during 1969 with the new P-350 and P-500 chassis offerings. There was also an Econoline mini-motorhome developed by an outside company but sold mainly through Ford dealers.

Ford dealers retailed more than 580,000 light trucks during 1969. It had been quite a decade for Ford, with retail sales nearly tripling. And better years were coming.

1970: SALES? WE'LL SHOW YOU SALES!

For the first year of the new decade, Ford Motor Company came on like gangbusters, launching an all-out assault on the heavy-duty truck segment. Its primary weapon: the Louisville Line, a series of all-new heavy-duty and severe service trucks that were destined to become legends. Built in Ford's massive new Louisville, Kentucky, truck plant—the biggest truck plant in the world—the new L-line truck series was comprised of LT-series tandem axle trucks that replaced the former T-series; LN-series short conventionals replacing the former N-series; L-series single-axle conventionals replacing the F-800 to F-1000 trucks, LNT short conventional tandem jobs, and the new LTS-series of setback-axle severe-duty tandem axle construction trucks. The new trucks offered three BBC dimensions. Both gas and diesel engines were available.

The new heavy-duty trucks were extraordinarily well engineered: they were lighter for better fuel economy, more maneuverable, quieter, and better riding than the trucks they replaced. To help fleet owners reduce operating costs, they were also designed for easier servicing.

At the other end of the spectrum was the restyled Ranchero, which advertising referred to as a "personal pickup." A new wood-sided Ranchero Squire model debuted this year with woodgrain side panels, full wheel discs, and whitewall tires, showing its emphasis on luxury rather than utility. The Ranchero GT was another highline version, this one geared toward muscle-car enthusiasts. The Bronco and Econoline models returned with only minor updates.

There was some news in the F-series light-truck lines. The company introduced new trim packages in the F-100 through F-350 models while also upgrading standard equipment. The Custom was now the base model, and above that were the Sport Custom, the Ranger, and the luxurious new Ranger XLT.

The combination of increased production available from the Ford truck plants along with bold new marketing efforts set Ford truck sales on fire in 1970 as the division handily outsold rival Chevrolet by more than 100,000 units. For the year, Ford captured some 38 percent of the light-truck market.

1971

To say the Ford truck line for 1971 was extensive would be an understatement; it reportedly consisted of more than 1,100 models and variations. But the trucks were mainly carryover this year with a host of improvements and styling updates. F-series trucks and Econoline

vans got new grilles and trim. Power brakes became standard equipment on F-250 and F-350 models. Broncos received upgraded front axles and heavier-duty front suspension. B-series school bus chassis got upgraded rear axles and larger batteries.

Ford's military truck operations developed a ½-ton postal delivery van this year, with a body produced by an Ohio company called Orrville Metal Products. Based on a 99-inch-wheelbase Ford chassis, the postal van was powered by the 250-cid inline six-cylinder engine hooked up to a fully automatic transmission. The company received an order from the US Postal Service for some eight thousand units. Final assembly was done at Ford's Highland Park factory.

Ford's light-truck sales inched upward to top 632,000 units for the calendar year.

1972: BREAKING ALL RECORDS

This year the Ford truck division entered the conventional compact pickup market (though some refer to it as the subcompact truck market) with a rebadged Mazda truck. Unlike the earlier Falcon-based Ranchero, the new Ford Courier was a smallish ½-ton truck imported from Japan. Powered by a Mazda 1,800cc four-cylinder engine mated to a 4-speed

This pretty green F-100 with the Styleside body is a 1972 model. This year Ford F-series trucks were mainly carryover but sold extremely well; the company's truck division set a new record for sales with more than 777,000 units delivered in the United States.

transmission, it proved surprisingly popular. F-series trucks were again mainly carryover for 1972, with some improvements to enhance capability. There was an all-new Ranchero this year and it was a beauty! Based on the new Torino, the Ranchero featured bold body sculpting, quad headlamps flanking a recessed grille, and a fast-sloping windshield, making this the sportiest-looking Ranchero yet.

Ford's Club Wagon in the Econoline series was given a new sliding side door to improve entry and exit; this door was a no-cost option on other E-series vans.

In the heavy-truck lines, new LT-880 and LNT-880 tandems were introduced. These low-priced heavies were created to compete with similar models from International, GMC, and Chevrolet. The W-series trucks got three new owner-operator dress-up packages.

In what proved to be a record-breaking year for the automotive industry, Ford dealers in 1972 sold more than 777,000 trucks in the United States—another new record for the division and a real achievement. Ford continued to hold first place in light-truck sales in the United States.

1973

This year was something of a milestone year for Ford, marking seventy years in business. It was also a milestone for Ford's truck business, with the company deciding to become a much larger factor in the recreational vehicle business. Campers, motorhomes, and converted (or upfitted) vans were the latest craze hitting America, and Ford wanted to earn a healthy share of that very profitable business. The company named its revamped truck operation the Truck and Recreational Vehicle Products Operations and gave it marching orders to become a bigger player in the pickup camper and motorhome chassis markets.

At the same time Ford extensively revised its F-series light-truck cabs and beds, along with incorporating longer wheelbases and frame-mounted fuel tanks. Front disc brakes became standard equipment on two-wheel-drive F-100 through F-350 models. In line with company goals to expand in the camper market, a new F-350 Super Camper model debuted with an 8-foot Styleside bed and a unique chassis designed especially for hauling a camper shell.

This year the medium-duty Ford F-500 through F-750 trucks switched to the same basic cab as the lower F-series trucks, albeit with needed modifications to suit their usage. The instrument panel, though, was carried over from the prior year.

There were other changes. Rancheros got new 5-mile-per-hour safety bumpers. The big LN and LNT trucks were given a new Cummins V-903 option. And the W-series trucks received an aerodynamically styled line-hauler with a streamlined front end for better fuel efficiency. The Bronco lineup shrank to just wagons as the slow-selling pickup went out of production. This year the 200-cid six became standard equipment.

Ford sold an incredible 897,227 light trucks for 1973, though in the end Chevrolet took the crown as top-selling light-truck line for the calendar year, a result of fielding a completely redesigned line of pickups. However, in October 1973 an event occurred that

would have far-reaching consequences for Chevrolet, Ford, and the entire automotive industry: the Organization of the Petroleum Exporting Countries—OPEC for short— announced an embargo on oil going to the United States to protest the country's support of Israel. The effects were sudden and sharp; in the months that followed, oil prices climbed rapidly from three dollars a barrel to twelve dollars a barrel, there were long lines at gasoline stations, and the US economy began to sink into recession. If either Ford or Chevrolet expected to see new sales records in 1974, they were about to be severely disappointed.

1974: WHERE'D ALL THE OIL GO?

As 1974 opened, the country was still reeling from the effects of the first gasoline shortages since World War II. In an effort to conserve fuel, the government announced a 55-mile-per-hour speed limit on highways, which would yield important fuel economy savings, though it proved unpopular with many self-important drivers who complained that it slowed them down too much.

The gas crisis had a devastating effect on truck sales as worried shoppers began to switch from purchasing trucks for personal use to buying small economical cars

ABOVE: Here's the Ford Bronco wagon for 1974, looking very much like it did in 1966 and having an increasingly harder time competing with the larger Chevy Blazer and Jeep Cherokee. Thankfully the SUV market was so hot that sales were still decent, but Ford management realized they would eventually need a larger Bronco.

LEFT: A new grille helps to identify the 1973 Ford F-series trucks. Shown here is an F-100 on the jobsite. Although it's used as a work truck, the owner ordered it with XLT trim, so it's probably his daily driver. Note the bright windshield moldings, rocker panel trim, and concave groove on the body sides, which replaced the convex form used the prior year. Although the F-series were greatly improved this year, the styling was similar to previous years.

instead. Sales of four-wheel-drive units were especially hurt because of their reputation as gas guzzlers. Pickup truck and sport utility vehicle sales began to slow dramatically. Once the economy began to soften, sales of heavy trucks also began to drop; fleets were reluctant to purchase because they couldn't be sure they would have enough business to justify buying new vehicles.

Caught unprepared, US automakers had little they could do but go ahead with new vehicle introductions already underway. There were many minor improvements to the heavy trucks for 1974, including heavier-duty axles available in the Louisville Line. In light trucks there were several powertrain changes to meet new emissions standards. The 300-cid six was now standard on E-series vans and optional on the F-100, while the massive 460-cid V-8 became available for both the E-100 and Ranchero. Broncos got minor interior changes but otherwise were carryover.

Midyear Ford introduced its new SuperCab pickups, which featured an extended rear section in the cab with room for extra passengers. It came in response to requests from buyers who were looking for pickups capable of carrying a family. With the SuperCab the rear section could be fitted with sideways-facing jump seats or a forward-facing bench seat. The new trucks were available with either a 6.75-foot or 8-foot Styleside bed.

Ford's light-truck sales fell to 780,000 for the year, and the trend was for a further drop in sales. In view of the poor shape of the economy, that was to be expected.

Talk about a "better idea"! In mid-1974 Ford introduced the new SuperCab truck models, which featured extra room behind the seats for stowing extra gear or carrying two extra passengers. This was a smart move on Ford's part because it helped buyers justify purchasing a truck instead of a car; they could now carry a small family within the cab.

1975

The fuel shortages in America began easing up this year, though the higher gasoline prices still seemed shocking to people who'd spent their entire lives paying less than thirty-five cents a gallon. The economy remained locked in a sharp recession. Companies were watching their hiring and capital expenditures, which, of course, further depressed the economy.

With thousands of unsold trucks parked on dealer lots across America, the automakers were forced to resort to rebates to move the merchandise. And although it worked, it was an extremely costly action and set a precedent the industry is still stuck with. Rebates, essentially unknown prior to this point, have since become a permanent feature for a large percentage of vehicle sales transactions.

There was an important new truck model, the F-150 ½-ton pickup, which was slotted in between the basic F-100 and the ¾-ton F-250. Although nominally rated as a ½-ton, the F-150 offered a payload capacity of 2,285 pounds, which was 550 pounds more than the F-100's maximum rating. Yet the F-150 offered the same good riding qualities of the F-100, and at a still-low price. Additional truck models added this year were new heavy-duty LN-600 through LN-750 models, along with P-450 and P-550 parcel delivery chassis.

Ford sold large numbers of the F-250 pickups, and they were especially popular with the XLT trim because it had nicer interior and exterior features at a moderate cost. It was also an easier way to dress up a truck—just check off the XLT box and most of the work was done for you. This is a 1975 model.

ABOVE: Created to display various ideas, this 1976 Custom F-100 has a few items added that really make it cool, including the Stepside body, black-painted grille, Magnum 500–style wheels, chrome bumper and mirror, and special striping. By this point the idea of a "sport truck" was catching on as America's love affair with trucks continued to blossom.

LEFT: By 1978 the venerable Ford C-series line was looking a bit long in the tooth, but they could be ordered with special paint to dress them up a little. These sturdy workhorses were still surprisingly popular despite having been on the market since 1957 with almost no styling changes.

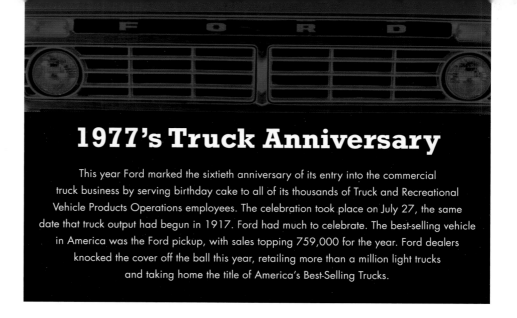

1977's Truck Anniversary

This year Ford marked the sixtieth anniversary of its entry into the commercial truck business by serving birthday cake to all of its thousands of Truck and Recreational Vehicle Products Operations employees. The celebration took place on July 27, the same date that truck output had begun in 1917. Ford had much to celebrate. The best-selling vehicle in America was the Ford pickup, with sales topping 759,000 for the year. Ford dealers knocked the cover off the ball this year, retailing more than a million light trucks and taking home the title of America's Best-Selling Trucks.

Perhaps the biggest news, though, was the introduction of all-new Econoline trucks with a bold new extended front end, clean styling, and new features. With the increased front overhand, Ford engineers were able to reduce engine intrusion into the passenger compartment for a quieter cabin with less heat generating through the floor hump. For the first time the new trucks also utilized body-on-frame design rather than unit-body and boasted longer wheelbases, redesigned suspensions, and revised steering systems. Power disc brakes were now standard equipment. The new instrument panel allowed for complete integration of the optional air conditioning controls and vents. Econoline vans and Club Wagons were also more luxurious than before; AM/FM stereo was now available, as were captain's chairs. Model numbers were revised to align with the company's pickup offerings, so the E-200 became the E-150, the E-300 became the E-250, and the heavy-duty job was the E-350.

At the same time, the medium-duty models were upgraded with improvements to the gasoline engine offerings. Heavy-duty trucks were given antiskid systems in line with a new federal requirement on air brakes. The new rules went into effect on March 1.

1976

As the new year opened there was good news—the economy was rebounding sharply and vehicle sales were on the rise. The sales increases were greatest in the truck segment, with light-truck sales rising to a new industry record. At Ford, sales were climbing nicely, though affected by a United Automobile Workers strike that lasted four weeks.

The smallest Ford trucks, the Japanese-built Courier pickups, were redesigned this year with a larger cab, more interior room, and upgraded interior trim. A 5-speed manual transmission was now available, along with soft-ride suspension and AM/FM radio.

To continue to grow its momentum in the marketplace, Ford gave its F-series trucks some appearance changes this year: a new grille and revised exterior trim, along with the addition of a new "Shorty Flareside" sport truck with a 6.5-foot bed. There were also several special edition packages for 1976, such as the XLT Luxury, the Bicentennial Option Group, and the cruising van.

Changes to the Econoline series were minor; the company couldn't build enough to meet the incredible demand for them so they decided to keep things simple and not introduce any substantial changes.

The big-truck series added a new top-line model, the LTL-9000 tandem-axle long-nose conventional with a 118.3-inch BBC. The drivetrain included a Cummins diesel matched to a Roadranger 10-speed gearbox.

All these changes and improvements helped push Ford light-truck sales past the 900,000 mark for the calendar year.

1977: LOOKS LIKE A MILLION

The sport-utility market was growing by leaps and bounds by this point, but Ford—and rival International—were selling smaller SUVs that struggled to compete with the larger, plusher units from Chevrolet, Jeep, and GMC. The Bronco was showing its age, and all Ford could do this year was upgrade its standard equipment and introduce dress-up packages in hopes they would help attract buyers. But management realized that a new, larger Bronco was needed and had its stylists and engineers working on one.

Along those lines, Ford announced midyear a reengineered F-250 4x4 regular-cab pickup with a lowered ride height for easier entry and exit, along with greatly improved handling.

There was a revamped Ranchero this year. Built on the revised Ford LTD II passenger car, it featured angular styling marked by massive bumpers, stacked rectangular headlamps, and a pseudo-Mercedes grille. The Ford Courier line now offered a choice of long- or short-wheelbase models.

The last of the old Y-block V-8s were phased out this year and replaced by truck versions of the 351-cid and 400-cid passenger-car engines. The reason was the newer engines were lighter, cost less, and provided important fuel economy improvements.

The old P-350 and P-400 parcel delivery chassis were dropped this year, replaced by versions of the Econoline E-250 and E-350. The M-series motorhome chassis were likewise dropped. There was a good deal of model consolidation and rationalization in the medium-truck lines.

In a continuing effort to jazz up its light-truck lines, Ford introduced new aluminum wheel options, appearance packages, and special models, including a new freewheeling package for F-series trucks and Econoline vans.

1978

The new year marked Ford's seventy-fifth year in business, and the company was celebrating by introducing several new car and truck models. There was a big new Bronco based on the F-series platform and able to carry up to six passengers along

Just in time for Ford Motor Company's seventy-fifth anniversary came the big new Bronco SUV. It was just what the market wanted and was a hot seller right from the start. The SUV market had moved away from the smaller Commando/Scout style of SUVs and was embracing larger, softer units.

ABOVE: Nominally rated as a 1-ton truck, the Ford F-350 could be ordered with various suspension upgrades to haul a substantially greater payload. Equipped with a stake-and-platform body, these trucks were, and still are, popular with landscaping firms. This is a 1978 model.

RIGHT: The Ford Motor Company celebrated its seventy-fifth year in business during 1978. The F-series trucks, such as this F-100 Ranger, received a new grille and frontal appearance that gave them the look of the big Louisville Line trucks, bold and aggressive.

with their luggage. Riding a wheelbase that, at 104 inches, was a foot longer than the previous Bronco, it had a removable fiberglass roof. The standard engine was now a 351-cid V-8. A 400-cid V-8 was optional. The new Bronco was exactly what the public wanted, and sales were red-hot right from the start.

The Ranchero returned this year with only minor appearance changes, while the Econoline vans were given a facelift to update their styling. In January the Econoline series added longer Super Wagon and Super Van models, each with a 20-inch extension to the rear body.

F-series trucks got a facelift this year; their new grille and frontal appearance gave them the look of mini–Louisville Line trucks—very handsome indeed. A glamorous new Ranger Lariat version of the F-series pickups became the new top-line model in the series.

There was big news in the heavy-truck segment, where Ford unveiled its new CL-9000 cab-over, a replacement for the W-series. Available in five single-axle versions as

well as nine tandem-axle wheelbases, the new trucks were premium in every way. Power was provided by a choice of Cummins, Detroit Diesel, and Caterpillar engines.

With the substantial help of the new Bronco and restyled F-series, Ford light-truck sales surged past the 1,264,000 mark for 1978, establishing a new record and pouring substantial profits into the venerable firm.

1979: SO LONG, SHAH— HELLO, ANOTHER GAS CRISIS!

For Ford Motor Company, the 1979 model year started off well. The company introduced a new advertising slogan, "Built Ford Tough," that proved very popular with buyers.

The little Ford Courier looked about the same this year, but under the hood was a larger, more powerful 2.0-liter four-cylinder engine. Two Courier models were offered: pickup or cab and chassis.

ABOVE: The medium-duty Ford F-600 was strictly a work truck—and a great one at that. This 1978 model has the new front bumper used on all the F- and B-series 600 through 800 models. Note the West Coast-style mirrors needed to see around the stake body.

During the 1979 model year, Ford introduced a new advertising slogan that was destined to last: "Built Ford Tough." It proved very popular with buyers and was used in various forms for years. Rectangular headlamps became standard equipment on F-series trucks this year. The pretty truck shown here is a 1979 F-150 Lariat.

The Ranchero was once again carried over with no significant styling changes and, sad to say, this would be its final year. The popularity of car-based pickups had fallen, and it didn't make economic sense to redesign a new one. The Bronco carried over with few changes as well, though in its case it was simply that it was so new—and selling so well—there wasn't much need for alterations. Econoline vans got a new grille this year and new rectangular headlamps.

Rectangular headlamps became standard equipment on the F-series trucks this year as the US auto industry continued its move to the more modern-looking lamps.

The economy was in good shape and sales were humming along until midyear. Then in November 1978 oil workers in Iran went on strike to protest the government, leading to reduced oil production. In early 1979 the country's leader, the Shah of Iran, was forced to flee amid large protest rallies against his autocratic rule. The resulting civil unrest in Iran caused oil production to further plummet, and by year's end oil exports were halted. This in turn created a new panic in world oil markets, fueling another dramatic rise in oil prices.

Once again the US economy was battered by the fuel shortages and once again truck sales began to drop. Ford trucks sales fell by about two hundred thousand units for the year, but what the future would bring was unknowable. Things, however, did not look good.

Chapter 7

TROUBLED TIMES

Ford Motor Company had earlier scheduled a redesign of its medium-duty trucks for 1980, endowing them with styling that was similar to the big Louisville Line heavy trucks so, despite the sinking US economy, the revised mediums were unveiled to the market. Using the corporate cab mated to new front-end sheet metal, they were good-looking and well-built trucks; it was simply their misfortune to be introduced at the start of another recession. This one would prove severe, too, because it featured an unusual combination of high inflation and a stagnant economy, a rare condition that became known as "stagflation."

Heavier-duty than the F-100 but still in the light-truck category is this 1980 F-150 Custom 4x4 pickup with a stylish shortbed, spoke wheels, and stripes. During the year, the US economy continued to falter, with high inflation coupled with high unemployment, and as a result truck sales began to drop.

The downturn affected sales of the Econoline Custom vans, including both the numerous aftermarket jobs and the factory-produced Customs. Rising prices of fuel and vehicles created a double whammy that put many younger people—the ones who usually bought cruising vans and compact trucks—out of the market.

In response to fuel economy concerns among SUV buyers, the Bronco this year was powered by a 300-cid six-cylinder engine as standard equipment, with a 302-cid V-8 also offered. A more efficient transfer case was also introduced. The Ford Courier trucks were carryover this year and it was no surprise—their sales had dwindled when buyers returned to larger vehicles. Ford was working on a replacement that would be a bit larger and much more appealing. In the heart of the market—the light-duty pickup truck end—the company fielded a revamped lineup. Ford called its heavily revised F-series "The First New Trucks of the 1980s." They boasted new sheet metal along with a distinctive new grille that incorporated large rectangles and a unique new headlamp/turn-signal arrangement. On the popular SuperCab models, new twin-pane rear side glass lent a more luxurious look to the vehicle. Inside, redesigned seats provided passengers with about 10 percent more room. Mechanically there was a new, more efficient transfer case on four-wheel-drive models, and fuel economy improvements in the engine line.

For the 1980 model year, Ford introduced a heavily revised F-series, calling them "The First New Trucks of the 1980s." The trucks were given new sheet metal, a grille with a distinctive rectangle design, and a unique headlamp/turn-signal combination. Shown here is a 1980 F-100 Ranger.

1981

The economy was slipping further downward as the 1981 model year opened, and all in all it was a bad time for a manufacturer to stand pat on its product lines. However, that's pretty much what Ford did with its light-truck lines. The F-series, Econoline, Courier, and Bronco were carried over with very little exterior changes, though there were numerous mechanical updates put though to improve quality, fuel economy, and drivability.

In the big-truck line, the company increased the number of seating options in order to accommodate buyers' specific needs. There were also improvements to the braking systems and clutches, new exterior color choices, and a broader range of rear-axle ratios.

In the end it wasn't enough to spark a revival in what was a very bad year economically, and Ford truck sales fell by about fifty thousand units for the year, in line with the overall market.

Ford Bronco for 1981 offered a 115-horsepower six-cylinder engine in addition to a choice of V-8 engines. The 130-horsepower 302-cid V-8 was standard equipment on Broncos sold in California, while the 156-horsepower 351-cid V-8 was optional on all Bronco models.

1982: THE BEST OF TIMES, THE WORST OF TIMES

This year Ford management responded to the ongoing recession—which had drastically cut truck sales—by pushing through some appearance changes to freshen its lineup. Bronco models were given a minor facelift to update their looks. The new grille included a blue oval Ford badge that replaced the former hood-mounted letters.

Like the Bronco, F-series trucks got a new grille with the blue oval badge. Mechanical improvements included lubed-for-life ball joints, as well as fuel economy gains. F-100s debuted a new 232-cid V-6 engine that produced 109 horsepower and 184 lb-ft of torque. California trucks now came with a 302-cid V-8 as standard. The Econoline series had no exterior appearance changes of note but got upgraded interior trim and a padded instrument panel.

A new F-700 four-wheel-drive truck was introduced to serve buyers needing an extra-duty off-road work vehicle. Also this year the LN-7000 trucks were given a Caterpillar 3208 diesel engine as standard equipment. Rated at 175 horsepower, it was a rugged, long-life workhorse engine. Steel-belted radial tires were now offered in the F-series heavy trucks.

Ford light-truck retail sales rose to 746,000 units this year. While it was encouraging to see an increase, truck sales were still down by more than half a million units compared to the record year of 1978.

Ford introduced its all-new American-made small pickup for 1982, naming it the Ranger, a longtime Ford model name. The Ranger replaced the Japanese-sourced Courier and outsold it by a huge margin. A great-looking, very versatile, and economical truck, it took the compact-truck market by storm.

What a great truck! This hefty F-350 crew cab, a 1983 model, sports optional two-tone paint for a jazzy style while still maintaining the capability to haul men, supplies, and tools from jobsite to jobsite with ease and comfort.

1983: SO LONG, OLD COURIER— HELLO, MR. RANGER!

This year the big truck news was all about a little truck—the all-new Ford Ranger compact pickup, which was replacing the long-in-the-tooth Courier. Although Ranger production actually had begun in January of 1982 in order to have trucks ready for sale in the second quarter, the new truck was considered an early 1983 model.

The Ranger was offered as a ½-ton pickup available in either two- or four-wheel drive, and offering two wheelbase lengths: 107.9 inches or 113.9 inches. Base power for two-wheel-drive models was a 2.0-liter four producing 73 horsepower while four-wheel-drive models came with a 2.3-liter four good for 79 horsepower. Optional was a 2.3-liter four producing 82 horsepower or a 2.2-liter diesel that generated 59 horsepower along with 90 lb-ft of torque and outstanding fuel economy.

Ford's F-series trucks carried over their own attractive styling with little change. Mechanical improvements included a new viscous fan clutch that helped improve fuel economy while providing a quieter engine, and the lineup expanded to include the addition of the new F-7000 and F-8000 models, which offered both single and tandem rear axle versions.

Helped by the popular new Ranger, Ford's light-truck sales continued their steady climb, topping the 950,000-unit mark this year.

ABOVE: The medium-duty F-350 stake truck for 1983 was one of the most popular work trucks in the world, with its combination of rugged durability and a value-oriented price tag. During the year, Ford retailed some 950,000 trucks in the United States.

OPPOSITE: Ford's popular LN-700 series was a heavy-duty truck designed for hard work. The 1983 model seen here would be a fairly typical example.

1984: TIPPECANOE AND BRONCO II

Just as the Ford F-series pickups spawned the big Bronco, for 1984 the Ford Ranger line spawned a new compact sport utility vehicle called, naturally enough, the Bronco II. It entered what was a rapidly growing market segment that heretofore had been dominated by Japanese trucks and the recently introduced Chevy S-10 Blazer. A two-door SUV with a standard V-6 engine, Bronco II was an immediate success.

The Ranger series carried over this year with little appearance change but began offering an optional V-6 engine that made it a much more capable off-roader, as well as giving it enough grunt to handle jobs such as heavy hauling and snowplowing.

The Ford F-100 was gone this year, a victim of increasingly difficult emissions regulations. Introduced in 1953, it had enjoyed an unusually long thirty-one-year model run. The F-150, introduced in 1975, became the new base model in the full-size F-series. Styling of the F-series trucks was carried over from the prior year.

Medium-duty Ford trucks this year offered an interesting new split brake system that combined the best features of hydraulic and air brakes into one low-cost package.

Ford light-truck sales came in at a very healthy 1.1 million units this year, proof that the economic downturn was over and a new era of prosperity was underway.

1985: THANKS A MILLION POINT TWO

Ford announced its big "Quality Is Job 1" commitment for 1985 in response to buyer complaints over the poor quality of American vehicles versus Japanese cars and trucks. Ford president Donald Peterson promised a "total quality approach" to the design, engineering, and assembly of Ford products. For America's automakers it was, in truth, long overdue. Quality had been on a downward path since the 1970s.

This year saw fuel injection debut on several truck engines, including the 5.0-liter (302-cid) V-8 in F-series and full-size Bronco models, as well as the 2.3-liter four in the Ranger. Ever-tightening emission regulations, along with the need to improve fuel economy and drivability, were forcing automakers to make the switchover from old-fashioned carburetors to modern fuel injection systems, and for most consumers it was a welcome change. Engines with fuel injection tended to start faster and run smoother. Fuel injection also reduced maintenance requirements.

Bronco II styling was carryover this year, which didn't seem to matter. Sales soared to nearly 100,000 units for the year. As good as that was, it was nothing compared to Ranger model year production of more than 230,000 units. This year Ranger added a stripped S-model priced at just $5,993, targeting the low-priced Asian trucks.

F-series trucks returned with little styling change for 1985 but offered minor mechanical updates. Ditto the Econoline series. For the year Ford retailed some 1.2 million light trucks in the United States.

The F-series medium and heavier trucks now boasted a new one-piece fiberglass tilt-hood option for easier servicing and reduced weight.

1986

Rival Chrysler Corporation had introduced a radical truck idea during 1984: a compact minivan aimed at families who needed (or thought they needed) a van in order to have enough room for passengers and cargo. The good-looking minivans soon proved to be among the hottest-selling trucks on the market, causing General Motors and Ford to scramble to come up with a competitive model. Chevy's answer was the Astro van, and for Ford it was the 1986 Aerostar, introduced in mid-1985. With boldly aerodynamic styling that shared nothing with the rest of the Ford truck lines, the Aerostar offered a choice of four-cylinder or V-6 power. But Ford flubbed in one key area: the Aerostar was a rear-drive minivan at a time when buyers were embracing front-wheel-drive minivans, such as the Dodge Caravan and Plymouth Voyager.

The Bronco II carried over with little appearance change this year, as did the big Bronco, Ranger, F-series, and Econoline. There was an exciting new SuperCab model in the Ranger lineup that was attracting a great deal of attention. By adding 17 more inches of passenger room to the cab, Ford engineers enabled small families to ride together in relative comfort despite the Ranger's compact size.

Also new this year was the Ford Cargo, a European-style tilt cab that had originally debuted in the UK. US models were built in Ford's Sao Paulo, Brazil, plant and shipped to

ABOVE: The F-150 SuperCab for 1985 was again very popular with families. The two-tone effect on this truck was particularly admired. Overall the Ford Motor Company reported excellent results for the year with truck sales of more than 1.2 million units in the United States.

RIGHT: For 1985 the F-series pickups saw little appearance change but were treated to the addition of an optional fuel-injected 5.0-liter 302-cid V-8 engine that developed 190 horsepower. The standard engine remained the carbureted 300-cid six-cylinder job, good for 115 horsepower. New emission regulations, along with the need to improve drivability, were forcing automakers to make the switchover from carburetors to fuel injection systems. Pictured here is a 1985 F-150.

Here We Go Again!

Also debuting during 1986 was the new Ford Cargo, a European-style tilt-cab medium-duty truck that had originally debuted in the UK. And in a repeat of what Ford management had done earlier with its compact Courier pickups, the new Cargo truck was imported rather than American-made. US-bound Cargo models were built in Ford's Sao Paulo, Brazil, plant and shipped to North America. Powered by a six-cylinder diesel, they were excellent trucks for city use. The carryover Ford C-series tilt-cab trucks continued in the line.

North America. Powered by a six-cylinder diesel, they were excellent trucks for city use. The carryover Ford C-series tilt-cab trucks continued in the line.

The heavy-duty line was now able to offer special savings on stock units available from Ford's Supply Center, a storage facility on the grounds of the big Kentucky Truck Plant. In addition, the CL and CLT models now offered new aftercooler systems on their diesel engines to boost power and improve durability.

It was another great year for Ford. According to published reports in industry trade magazines this year, the company sold over 1.3 million trucks in America.

1987

The first major update for the F-series trucks since 1980 was unveiled for the 1987 model year. All-new styling was more integrated and aerodynamic than previously and featured rounded front corners and a sleek new rectangular-theme grille flanked by rectangular headlamp/turn-signal units.

The big Bronco shared the new styling themes with the F-series trucks, giving them a more efficient, aerodynamic look. Rear-wheel anti-lock brakes were introduced to the F-series trucks, the Bronco, and the Bronco II. Fuel injection was now standard on all six-cylinder light-truck models.

According to Ford advertising, the new Ford trucks were "an investment in value" because they offered more standard features and greater durability than the competition.

The well-loved Ford C-series trucks celebrated thirty years in production this year, though the lineup was down to just three models due to reduced demand. The newer, more modern Cargo-series trucks were proving popular and doubtless were also stealing sales from the venerable C-series models.

Meanwhile, the Ford Ranger returned for the 1987 model year with only minor improvements and essentially no appearance changes. The full line of Ford trucks was advertised as "an investment in value" because they offered more standard features and greater durability than the competition.

The big Ford LTL-9000 conventional line-haul trucks—the glamour stars of the heavy-duty line—got a revised cabin and new instrument panel this year, along with improved Cummins and Cat engines. One choice, the Cummins Big Cam IV, offered up to 400 horsepower.

Sadly, Henry Ford II, the colorful Ford executive who first took control of the family business during World War II, died of pneumonia in September, at the age of seventy.

Ford Motor Company sold just under 1.4 million light trucks in the United States during 1987.

1988

Because the F-series trucks had been so thoroughly revamped the prior year, there were few changes in them for 1988. But thankfully the F-series trucks, senior Broncos, and Econolines now offered an optional fuel-injected, 351-cid V-8 pumping out 210 horsepower.

This year the public was once again calling for more power in their family vehicles, so the Ford Aerostar dropped its standard four-banger in favor of the 3.0-liter V-6. Three Aerostar models were offered for 1988: cargo van, window van, and wagon.

ABOVE: The husky L-8000 Class 8 trucks were Ford's hardest-working trucks, and they were often used for severe-duty jobs, including operating as snowplows and construction trucks. The 1988 model here is a prime example of where the slogan "Ford Tough" came from.

OPPOSITE: For the final year of the decade, Ford carried over the F-150 with only minor changes. None were really needed; the Fords had great styling and engineering and the broadest model range in the industry. This is a 1989 F-150 regular cab.

The Bronco II was mostly unchanged this year but added a high-trim XL Sport package to its offerings. The Ford Ranger still came with a standard four-cylinder engine because that was what the market called for, but the optional V-6 engine was a very popular choice among buyers.

Ford introduced new Super Duty chassis-cab models with a 14,500-pound GVWR, slotted in between the regular 1-ton line and the F-600 medium jobs to offer buyers a lighter medium product. This year the company also dropped the medium-duty F-7000, F-8000, and FT-8000 models from the lineup, along with the B-7000.

The cabs on Ford's big Class 7 and Class 8 trucks this year featured greater use of galvanized steel to prevent early rusting and also benefited from a $24 million investment in the plant's paint system. A new LN-7000 model was introduced, sort of a cross between a heavy-duty and medium-duty truck. New heavy-duty versions of the Cargo line were also unveiled.

Ford retailed nearly 1.5 million trucks during the year.

1989

The truck market contracted a bit in 1989, though it was still an excellent year. Ford had some new products to show and that helped it turn in one of its best years ever.

The Aerostar minivan added two new versions in midyear, extended-length versions of its cargo van and window van models. Adding 15.4 inches to the overall length, the longer vans provided much more carrying room than before.

Ford Ranger and Bronco II models got redesigned front-end sheet metal this season along with new grille and exterior ornamentation. This year the Bronco II base model was the XL, while the upgrades in trim were the XL Sport, XLT, XLT Plus, and the top-end Eddie Bauer. Ranger trim levels of S, S Plus, Custom, GT, XLT, and STX were carried over from the previous year.

F-series trucks carried over with minor changes, as did the medium-duty units. The heavy-duty trucks now offered the new Caterpillar ATAAC engine series.

In this final year of the decade, Ford sold 1.4 million light trucks in the United States, a solid—and solidly profitable—number. The company was well poised to continue its dominant position in the industry.

Brawny enough for the toughest jobs were the Ford F-900 Super Duty trucks for 1989. The Super Duty line helped make Ford the most popular truck maker in America; they sold extremely well. During the calendar year Ford retailed an astonishing 1.4 million trucks in the United States.

1990 to 2008

GLORY DAYS

The year 1990 was historic for Ford in at least one sense because it marked the final year for the venerable Ford C-series cab-over trucks. First launched as a 1957 model, the C-series truck had retained its original styling since then and for most of those years was one of Ford's more popular trucks. To replace it, Ford began producing the Cargo line in the United States. Also in 1990, Ford called its products "Workforce Trucks."

Aerostar debuted six new four-wheel-drive versions this year—regular and extended cargo van, window van, and wagon models—featuring an electronically controlled all-wheel-drive system hooked up to a new 4.0-liter V-6 engine boasting multiport fuel injection. In all there were twelve distinct Aerostar models this year.

There was not much visual change in the Ford F-350 for 1990. Shown here is one of the most popular versions, the SuperCab with XLT trim. Note this truck is a "duallie," meaning it has dual rear wheels. The F-350's heavy-duty chassis and powerful engine made it ideal for towing.

Not surprisingly, this year the relatively fresh Ford F-series and Bronco II models had little appearance change, though a new 4-speed automatic overdrive transmission was now available, which boosted fuel economy and engine life while providing a much quieter engine at highway speeds. Econoline trucks were likewise little changed this year but were given expanded availability of the 4-speed automatic transmission.

Going for more volume, this year the Ranger series added a new S model with the Styleside bed, base priced at $8,646, about $1,400 lower than the regular Styleside model. The S model was offered only in a single two-wheel-drive version.

In the medium-duty range Ford added a low-profile F-600 model with a loading height of just 32 inches, half a foot lower than other models. Later on a low-profile F-700 joined the line.

Ford Motor Company retailed an impressive 1,373,493 light trucks in the United States this year.

1991: THE YEAR OF THE EXPLORER

The 1991 model year was one of the most exciting for Ford because this year it launched an all-new compact sport utility vehicle to challenge the almighty Jeep Cherokee. Both Ford and GM made a mistake when they first entered the compact SUV market with only two-door models. Thus, even though they fielded their entries well before Jeep, once the two- and four-door Cherokee XJ debuted it became one of the most coveted vehicles in America. With more room and easier entry/exit, Cherokee became the SUV to beat. For 1991 Ford was determined to knock Cherokee down a few pegs. It did this with its new Explorer, which was larger than the Cherokee, roomier, and offered both two- and four-door models, with or without four-wheel drive. Their introduction created a sensation—they soon became the hottest-selling compact SUVs in the country. Ford produced more than 320,000 in its first year, and with the introduction of the Explorer, the Bronco II was dropped.

There wasn't much new in the big Bronco line, though a Silver Anniversary model was offered this year to commemorate twenty-five years of Bronco sales.

Likewise the F-series trucks were mainly unchanged. The company unveiled an interesting new "Nite" blackout trim package that gave the trucks a dark, super cool appearance. As far as the rest of the F-series, since it was already the best-selling vehicle in America, Ford didn't need to change much to keep people happy, though the usual minor trim alterations were seen.

Ford Ranger was given a new Sport model for 1991, slotted in between the stripped S and the Custom series.

The big new Aeromax 120, launched this year, was claimed to be the most aerodynamically designed Ford heavy-duty truck ever. As stylish as it was, the Aeromax was a tough hauler and a fine testament to the Ford truck heritage. A total of 1,231,321 Ford light trucks were sold during the calendar year.

By 1992 Stepside-style pickups had long been out of fashion—except, that is, for sporty jobs such as this F-150 Flareside. With its stylish alloy wheels and body-color side steps, this was a young man's dream truck. Wouldn't you like to find one of these today?

1992

This was another big celebratory year for Ford trucks—the seventy-fifth anniversary of the company's entry into the truck market. This year Ford introduced an all-new lineup of Econoline trucks, their first complete redesign since 1975. The new Econolines were much sleeker and aerodynamic than previous versions, and had stylishly sculpted sides, a longer hood, and an egg-crate grille flanked by integrated halogen headlamps. Inside was an

ergonomically designed instrument panel that did away with the stripped "fleet van" look of prior vans. The new Econoline solidified Ford's dominant position in the full-size van market.

In the minivan field, the Aerostar got a new instrument panel to accommodate a driver-side air bag, along with a change in the placement of the shifter for the automatic transmission—it was up on the steering column now.

The Ranger was back with only minor powertrain updates and a few trim changes, and the Explorer carried over with only minor updates.

The hot-selling F-series trucks got a facelift this year, the new six-slot grille featuring two horizontal bars and two vertical bars flanked by aerodynamic headlamps. There was also a newly designed instrument panel.

Ford's well-respected medium-duty low-profile line was increased to four models offering a choice of seven wheelbases. Heavier-duty axles provided GVWRs of up to 28,000 pounds and a choice of hydraulic or air braking.

The Aeromax line was expanded this year, with the new Aeromax 106 and Aeromax 8000 models, and both offered a choice of day cab or sleeper cab versions. Ford sold 1.4 million trucks this year in the United States.

ABOVE: The 1992 Ford Bronco seen here is equipped with the highly desirable Eddie Bauer trim. Note the rear roof color and the lower-body cladding, as well as the huge alloy wheels and tires. This year marked Ford's seventy-fifth year in the truck market.

PREVIOUS PAGES: Another 1992 F-150, this one is a Lariat XLY equipped with the Nite package, alloy wheels, and raised white letters on the tires. By this point, style and sporty accessories were among the predominant features buyers looked for in pickups. Although many bare-bones work trucks were still being sold, they tended to go mostly to commercial buyers.

1993

For 1993 the senior Bronco dropped its standard six-cylinder engine in favor of a standard 302-cid V-8. The 351-cid V-8 remained optional. Econolines returned with little change but after such a complete overhaul the year before, none was expected.

Ford Explorers this year were given an anti-lock braking system (ABS) as standard equipment, a sign of a major movement in vehicle safety that was underway. Driver-side air bags and, in some case, passenger-side air bags, were coming into broad usage in America. Scoffed at by some, the move would save tens of thousands of lives in the end. The Explorer also added a premium Limited model this year, equipped with every conceivable luxury, to compete with the new Jeep Grand Cherokee that was a hot new entry in the market.

The 1993 Ranger pickups were completely redesigned this year and a very successful job it was. As America's best-selling compact pickup, the Ranger was lavished all the attention it deserved, gaining all-new sheet metal. The new look was, as expected, rounder and more aerodynamic while retaining a tough, rugged appearance. An interior upgrade was also introduced.

In the F-series there were some changes in models, with the Flareside box now available in XL and XLT versions and some name changes.

During the year Ford sold more than 1.6 million light trucks.

Although crew-cab pickups had long been available—International Harvester had one in the 1960s—they still hadn't really caught on with families yet, and certainly not to the extent they have today. Mostly they were ordered on heavier-duty trucks, such as this 1993 F-350 XLT, and were used to tow camping trailers or boats.

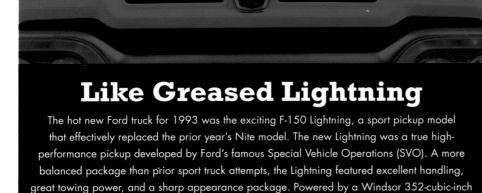

Like Greased Lightning

The hot new Ford truck for 1993 was the exciting F-150 Lightning, a sport pickup model that effectively replaced the prior year's Nite model. The new Lightning was a true high-performance pickup developed by Ford's famous Special Vehicle Operations (SVO). A more balanced package than prior sport truck attempts, the Lightning featured excellent handling, great towing power, and a sharp appearance package. Powered by a Windsor 352-cubic-inch V-8 pumping out 204 horsepower, the Lightning could accelerate zero to sixty in a mere 7.2 seconds, and do a quarter-mile in 15.6 seconds. Ford produced 5,276 units; of these some 2,691 were black and 2,585 were red.

RIGHT: A roomy SuperCab passenger compartment matched to a commodious cargo box can make for a long truck, as we can see with the attractive 1993 F-150 SuperCab shown here. Regardless of their large size—or perhaps even because of it—these were very popular trucks.

BELOW: Compare the previous photo of the longbed Crew cab with this one of a 1993 F-150 shortbed regular-cab pickup and you'll notice there's quite a difference in overall length. This particular truck is a four-wheel-drive model and was specified with the popular XLT trim.

The Most Famous
Ford Bronco of All Time

For 1994 there wasn't much that was new on the Ford Bronco. The series was
given a driver-side air bag this year and that was about it. However, despite that lack of
change, Bronco was probably the most talked about sport utility vehicle on the planet during
the year, or at least one Ford Bronco was. That was the white Ford Bronco that murder suspect
O.J. Simpson used in his bizarre flight from the police, which was watched on television by
millions of viewers around the globe. As O.J. drove down a California highway as if on his
way to the senior citizens' center, except for the dozens of police cars and helicopters following
his every move, it's difficult to imagine exactly how Simpson thought he might escape. Accused
of murdering Nicole Brown Simpson and Ron Goldman, O.J. Simpson would later
be found not guilty after one of the most controversial trials of the century.

1994

For 1994 the Ford Aerostar got a new Eddie Bauer model with four bucket seats, along
with new colors and a new high-mounted stoplight for the rear. Other than that there were
a few minor trim changes.

Ditto the Explorer. Ford was selling every unit it could build so there was little incentive
to introduce anything new. Ford factories this year pumped out more than 345,000
Explorers, making it the top-selling compact SUV by a huge margin.

The Ford Ranger got new side-guard door beams this year, and in the medium-duty
market the Kentucky Truck Plant began preproduction-building of a new Louisville Line of
mediums and heavies.

Also for 1994 the Econoline was given rear-wheel ABS on most models, with four-
wheel ABS for RV and camper chassis.

In a safety move, Ford's popular F-150 and F-250 models were given driver-side air
bags for 1994, along with side-guard door beams. The F-series continued its reign as
the best-selling vehicle in North America. This year Ford also boasted the best-selling car
(Taurus), compact pickup (Ranger), full-size van (Econoline), and compact SUV (Explorer).
It was a fantastic year for the automaker.

Late in the year Ford opened up a new Commercial Truck Vehicle Center in Dearborn,
Michigan, to facilitate the design, engineering, and marketing of commercial trucks on a
worldwide basis. An important part of a greater program called "Ford 2000," the center's
aims were reducing costs while improving the product and speeding up development. A
reported 1.8 million Ford light trucks were retailed during the calendar year.

OPPOSITE TOP: Ford was famous for
offering the broadest range of trim
and options in the business, which
its buyers very much appreciated. A
careful check-off of the options list
could yield a very special, individual-
looking truck, such as this 1994
F-150 with XLT trim, sport wheels,
body-color side steps, and a Flareside
build. Neat!

OPPOSITE BOTTOM: Sales of
conversion vans, while down from
their all-time peak, were still strong
when this pair of 1994 Club Wagon
conversions were produced. The van
in the foreground is an extended-body
Econoline while the white van in the
rear is a standard-length Econoline.
These vans were popular with
tailgaters and families that traveled
a lot, and they were usually outfitted
with the buyer's choice of a range of
seating options.

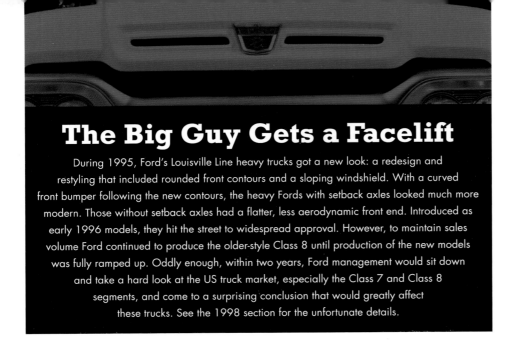

The Big Guy Gets a Facelift

During 1995, Ford's Louisville Line heavy trucks got a new look: a redesign and restyling that included rounded front contours and a sloping windshield. With a curved front bumper following the new contours, the heavy Fords with setback axles looked much more modern. Those without setback axles had a flatter, less aerodynamic front end. Introduced as early 1996 models, they hit the street to widespread approval. However, to maintain sales volume Ford continued to produce the older-style Class 8 until production of the new models was fully ramped up. Oddly enough, within two years, Ford management would sit down and take a hard look at the US truck market, especially the Class 7 and Class 8 segments, and come to a surprising conclusion that would greatly affect these trucks. See the 1998 section for the unfortunate details.

1995

Ford's product actions for 1995 acknowledged a hard fact—its Aerostar minivan hadn't proved strong-enough competition to the segment-leading Chrysler minivans. To correct that situation this season, Ford introduced a new minivan that it felt certain would be able to take on the Chrysler products; they called it the Windstar. It had front-wheel drive, as the market demanded, and it was long and sleek and attractive. Sharing some mechanical bits with the Taurus, the Windstar was powered by a 3.0-liter six on the base Cargo and GL models and a more potent 3.8-liter V-6 on the fancier LX version. Actually introduced in March 1994 as an early 1995 model, the Windstar achieved early success in the marketplace, with more than 160,000 produced for the year.

Surprisingly, the Aerostar remained in production for another two years as a lower-priced alternative; family models were priced about two thousand dollars less than the Windstar series.

F-series trucks were mainly carryover this year, though a sharp new Eddie Bauer model was introduced.

The Explorer was restyled for 1995 but arrived late in the season, being introduced in January. The front end was facelifted with new sheet metal that displayed a more pronounced slope to the hood and fenders, a rounder grille, and rounder headlamps. A new independent front suspension provided a smoother, quieter ride along with better handling, though of course at a loss of some of its off-road capability. It didn't matter all that much, however, since research showed most people never took their SUVs off-road.

The Bronco got a few changes this year, including a new XLT Sport model and integrated entry steps on the Eddie Bauer version. Econoline vans got a new drivers-side air bag, and the RV stripped chassis was dropped from the lineup.

Ranger pickups got a new interior this year, along with a new instrument panel shared with the Explorer. On the exterior there was a revised grille. Mechanically there was a

PREVIOUS PAGES: There was little change in appearance on the lighter F-series trucks for 1994, but the F-150 and F-250 models were given driver-side air bags for 1994, along with side-guard door beams. Ford continued to reign as the best-selling truck line in America.

RIGHT: Notice how much more aerodynamic-looking this 1997 F-250 SuperCab longbed pickup looks compared to the previous model years. The softer lines and lack of loud exterior striping give it a classy (rather than brassy) appearance. These all-new trucks were initially unveiled in January 1996 and began appearing in dealer showrooms that spring.

Adios, Big Guys!

Ford management reached a big decision in 1997. With resources scarce and the cost of product development high, it was time for Ford to focus all of its attention on its core markets—cars and light and medium trucks. Thus, it was decreed that the company would abandon the Class 8 market. It was a tough decision because the Class 8 segment was the glamour spot in the big truck market. But Ford officials reasoned that the company would be able to cover Class 1 through 3 with the F-150 series and much of the medium-duty market with variations of its bigger F-series trucks. The company had a huge investment in its big trucks and was able to find a buyer pretty easily. Daimler-Benz, maker of Mercedes-Benz and Freightliner trucks, purchased the Ford product line and renamed it Sterling, reviving an historic old truck name that few people remembered. If you look at any of the modern Ford-based Sterling trucks, you'll notice the "S" badge is oval-shaped, designed that way in order to fit the previous oval "Ford" badge slot. This transition marked the end of the line for the biggest Ford trucks, and Sterling itself was dropped by Daimler-Benz in March 2009.

new electronically controlled 4-speed automatic transmission for smoother shifts and improved fuel efficiency.

Ford's F- and B-series trucks were given new frames this year, and the F-series mediums got a facelift as well. The new Louisville Line of heavy-duty trucks went into regular production as 1996 models and were well received.

Ford light-truck sales rose to more than 1.9 million this year.

1996

For 1996 the Windstar closed-side cargo van was dropped, though the window version remained available. Power output of the Windstar's 3.8-liter V-6 was boosted to 200 horsepower via a new split-port induction system, and traction control was a new option.

The Explorer carried over with minor changes to engine availability plus a few new colors. The Bronco and Econoline likewise had a few minor upgrades but otherwise carried over unchanged.

Ford Ranger pickups had an interesting new feature this year: a passenger-side air bag with a key-operated shut-off switch so that the bag could be disabled when desired. On most vehicles back then both air bags would deploy whenever there was a frontal collision, a situation that could prove deadly to a child seated up front in an infant seat. The shut-off allowed a parent to disable the passenger-side bag for safety's sake.

There were no significant changes made to the F-series; Ford had an all-new model coming out early in the year and was waiting for that to unveil new features.

Seen here is a hard-working 1997 F-350 crew-cab pickup. This particular truck is a duallie, with flared rear fenders to enclose its big wheels and tires, along with dressed-up heavy-duty wheels, roof-mounted cab lamps, and trailer-type side mirrors. Fitted out for heavy towing jobs, it's equipped with Ford's torquey Power Stroke diesel engine.

1997

The F-series trucks were all new for the 1997 model year, and they appeared in showrooms months earlier than usual. Unveiled at the Detroit Auto Show in January 1996, they began to stream into Ford dealerships by early spring, about six months earlier than usual. Featuring a gently sloping hood line, rounded grille, and flush windshield, the new F-series looked so slick and aerodynamic that some wags began calling them "Taurus pickups." Yet for all their handsome looks, the new Ford trucks were as rugged and dependable as ever—probably more so. The company focused its early production efforts on the so-called "family" units, the SuperCab versions, which were popular and more profitable than the stripped work trucks. But as production ramped up smoothly, all models became available.

The big Bronco was dropped this year in recognition that the day of the full-size two-door sport utility vehicle had ended. But Ford had its replacement right at hand, an all-new SUV called the Expedition. Based on the F-series, the Expedition was similar in concept to

For the 1997 model year, Ford designers took a big chance with the appearance of the all-new F-series trucks, endowing them with smooth, aerodynamic lines that made them more fuel efficient and modern-looking than before, but which also made them look a bit smaller. Although they sold extremely well, apparently not everyone was pleased with the new styling. Critics soon dubbed them the "Taurus pickups," a reference to Ford's hot-selling aerodynamic midsize passenger cars.

the Chevy Suburban. F-series front sheet metal was used, though with a unique grille, and only a single four-door wagon body-style was offered. A 4.6-liter V-8 hooked up to a 4-speed automatic transmission was the standard powertrain, with a hefty 5.4-liter V-8 optional. Prices started at just under $28,000.

Windstar models carried over unchanged this year because the company had a freshened Windstar debuting as an early 1998 model. Aerostar got a new 5-speed automatic transmission for the 4.0-liter engine in this, its final year.

Explorers now offered the 4.0-liter six, solely with the optional 5-speed automatic, which made for a compact SUV with plenty of power and decent fuel economy. The automatic overdrive helped quiet engine noise at highway speeds.

This year the Flareside box could be ordered on any short-wheelbase Ranger model.

1998: HAS IT REALLY BEEN FIFTY YEARS?

Ford launched a revised Windstar in January 1997 as an early 1998 model. For all the hoopla surrounding it, changes were limited mainly to revised front-end styling, a 6-inch-longer driver-side door, and extra sound-deadening materials to quiet the cabin.

The Explorer got some changes as well, but these focused on the rear of the truck,with a new liftgate, rear bumper, and taillamps appearing. Ford Expeditions carried over unchanged.

Ranger pickups got several revisions and improvements for 1998, including new front-end styling, a lightweight aluminum hood, a 3-inch-longer cab on regular cab models, and a new front suspension. Rangers also got a new 2.5-liter engine to replace the aging 2.3 that had been around since the early 1970s. Offering three wheelbases (112-inch, 118-inch, and 125-inch), Rangers managed to appeal to a broad spectrum of buyers. The company also offered a handful of battery-powered electric Rangers for sale.

This year marked the fiftieth anniversary of the F-series trucks, but because the vehicles were all new the previous year, improvements this year were minor.

Ford Tough at King Ranch

There's a good reason why Ford chose to plant the King Ranch name on one of its trucks;
it's because King Ranch, like Ford, is as legendary, iconic, and American as you can get. The
famed Texas ranch is huge (825,000 acres) and it processes thousands of head of cattle, has
extensive farming operations, makes leather goods, raises some of the finest quarter
horses in the world, and also owns a hardware store and a publishing company,
not to mention huge citrus operations in Florida.

With tasks that can take a work crew more than 100 miles across the ranch on
any given day, hauling heavy equipment and tools, King Ranch's truck of choice is, as one
might expect, the Ford Super Duty. The Ranch operates about two hundred Ford trucks.

1999

The 1999 model year was one of mostly minor changes in the Ford light trucks. Windstar models finally got an available drivers-side sliding passenger door—Chrysler had one much earlier—and it was standard on SE and SEL models but an extra cost on the base and LX versions. The Explorer got a new front bumper, and Econoline E-150s now had four-wheel disc brakes as standard equipment.

The Ranger Splash model was dropped, leaving just the XL and XLT trim lines. However, the Ranger SuperCab models now featured two rear half (or pocket) doors, a huge improvement.

F-150s and F-250 SuperCabs also got two small rear doors this year, along with new grilles and front bumpers. The SVT Lightning now boasted a supercharged 5.4-liter engine banging out a whopping 360 horsepower.

As part of its consolidation program, Ford spun off the heavier-duty F-series trucks into their own separate category this year called the Super Duty line. It wasn't simply a marketing move either; the Ford Super Duty vehicles—F-350 and heavier—were all new this year. Introduced in the spring of 1998 as early 1999 models, the Super Duty trucks represented the company's drive to establish Ford as the dominant player in the medium-duty truck market. Besides the F-350 Super Duty, there were F-450 (1¼-ton) and F-550 (1½-ton) models. All were powered by Triton V-8s, in 5.4-liter and 6.8-liter versions, or a Power Stroke turbodiesel.

2000

For the first year of the new millennium, Ford made a big splash in the truck market by introducing a huge new SUV called the Excursion. It was aimed at people looking for a larger, heavier-duty tow vehicle, though of course it appealed also to people who need to drive a big vehicle to feel better about themselves. A 5.4-liter V-8 was standard equipment on this premium SUV, and prices began at $29,655 for the XLT base model and climbed to $39,635 for the Eddie Bauer model.

Other Ford models for 2000 received minor changes. Ford Windstar cargo vans were upgraded with a standard 3.8-liter V-6 this year. Explorers got some new colors and a shuffling of trim levels, and Expeditions got a few new items added to the options list. In the Econoline series, four-wheel ABS became standard equipment on E-150 models.

Explorers continued to come in both two-door and four-door models, though sales of the two-door lagged the four-door quite a bit, proving that the four-door model was the one consumers now preferred.

There were no changes in the basic configurations of the F-150s, but an exciting new Harley-Davidson model was introduced to widespread admiration; it was a great-looking truck. Available only as a two-wheel-drive Flareside SuperCab pickup with a short box, the Harley's drivetrain included a 5.4-liter V-8 hooked up to an automatic overdrive transmission. Exterior features included a unique grille, badging, black body paint, and five-spoke alloy wheels. A modified exhaust did its best to imitate the snarling sound of a Harley-Davidson motorcycle.

Since the F-250 Super Duty became available in late 1999, the F-150 ¾-ton model was dropped.

Sports trucks were increasingly popular, and Ford decided to bring a new one to market that had guts and power to go with its great styling. The result was this 2001 F-150 SVT Lightning, with a SOHC 330-cid supercharged V-8 that pumped out 380 horsepower and a whopping 450 lb-ft of torque, obviously not for the faint of heart. Unlike many other sports trucks, the SVT also got a revised suspension for better handling and cornering.

2001

Ford introduced an all-new small SUV this year called the Escape. Slotted below the Explorer, the Escape was aimed at the popular Honda CRV and Toyota RAV4 competition, which dominated the small SUV market. Unlike those entries, the Escape offered an optional V-6 engine in addition to its standard four-cylinder. With good styling and performance, the Escape was an early success.

This year the Windstar was given a new "Personal Safety System" consisting of dual-stage front air bags, a crash severity sensor, seat belt pretensioners and energy management retractors, and a driver's seat position sensor, all aimed at reducing or eliminating injuries in a collision. In addition, a new SE Sport model was introduced with 16-inch wheels, rocker-panel cladding, and a rear spoiler.

Expeditions and Econolines were mainly carryover this year, while Rangers were given the 4.0-liter V-6 as a new option. The Excursion's 7.3-liter Power Stroke turbodiesel had its output boosted to 250 horsepower, and a six-disc in-dash CD player was now available.

There was little new on the Explorer for 2001; an all-new model was just around the corner so the company didn't bother much with the carryover version. Two-door models got some new sheet metal and suspension revisions.

Perhaps the biggest news this year was the new F-150 four-door SuperCrew pickup. With four full-size doors, it opened up the pickup market to larger families and made it easier for them to choose a truck over a passenger car. There was also a sharp new King Ranch model that was as luxurious as the name implied.

TOP LEFT: Here's the sleek and stylish F-150 for 2004 in the immensely popular SuperCab body style. Ford trucks continued to be America's first choice. This year Ford Motor Company was again awarded *Motor Trend* magazine's "Truck of the Year" award for the F-150 pickup.

One of the hottest-looking Ford trucks of the entire decade was this 2004 F-250 Harley-Davidson Edition, with an all-new red-and-black paint scheme that just screams for attention. With a powerful overhead-cam engine, the Harley-Davidson provided more than enough power to go along with its great styling.

2002

The new model year brought a complete redesign of the Explorer and it was a good one, with a 2.5-inch-wider stance and a 2-inch-longer wheelbase. New styling was more aggressive-looking, and improvements were made to reduce noise and vibration. A new independent rear suspension system also offered notable improvements to ride and handling. There were larger door openings, an available third seat and reverse sensing system, a bit more power and fuel economy, and a sharp new interior. All in all, it was a home run for Ford.

The Windstar line got additional safety equipment for 2002, including Ford's new AdvanceTrac interactive vehicle dynamics system, an early form of antiskid control that used the brake system to correct a vehicle's direction in order to avoid a skid.

Certain Ford vehicles were given updated frontal appearances, including the Windstar LX, which got a new fascia, and the Excursion, which got new crystalline headlamp lenses.

The Escape got some new colors this year and some additional standard equipment to make it even more competitive with the RAV4 and CRV.

The Expedition offered seating for up to nine people, along with a 4-ton towing capability and up to 100 cubic feet of cargo room. As before, both two-wheel-drive and four-wheel-drive versions were offered.

The F-150 line was carryover but with new items added to the list of standard equipment. The F-150 XL now had standard air conditioning, while King Ranch SuperCrew models got automatic climate control. An interesting FX4 off-road package was now available on XLT and Lariat 4x4 models.

Ford's F-250 and F-350 Super Duty models now included a 6-speed manual transmission as standard equipment with either a 5.4- or 6.8-liter V-8.

2003

The Ford Motor Company celebrated a major milestone during 2003—the centennial of its founding by a small group of investors who for some reason had complete faith in Henry Ford's ability to design and engineer an automobile that would be a market success. Most of those early investors had made a fortune on that faith.

For the 2003 model year Ford unveiled a special Heritage Edition F-150 model with two-tone paint, special interior treatments, and special "1903–2003 Heritage Edition" badges. The F-150 Harley-Davidson model also got special anniversary-edition badges marking the centennial of Harley-Davidson, which also was founded in 1903. There was also a special edition F-150 STX offered in both standard cab and SuperCab models. It boasted a monochromatic theme with grille, bumpers, lower fascia, and wheel-lip moldings all painted the body color.

The Ford Expedition was redesigned this year, with clean new styling and the industry's first power-folding third-row seat. Available options now included an antiskid control system and side-curtain air bags.

2004

Ford continued to dominate the truck market for 2004, with the F-series trucks soldiering on as America's favorite vehicle by a wide margin. This year the F-series was completely redesigned, with a bigger, bolder look; more interior room; and greater capability. In this, its eleventh generation, the F-150 shared some styling cues with the bigger Ford trucks. With a wider stance, the F-150 looked tougher than before, and with a deeper cargo bed, it could carry more volume. In a major innovation this year, all cab styles included four doors; they were full-size doors on the SuperCrew, half-doors on the SuperCab, and

ABOVE: Another look at America's best-selling vehicle, the Ford F-series truck. Seen here is a rather typical F-series SuperCab longbed. This one has been ordered as a work truck with a minimum of exterior dress-up items. It's a 2004 model.

RIGHT: Ford's Super Duty series are its hardest-working trucks, tough vehicles that compete in the medium-duty segment. This big F-650 XLT chassis is built to handle a heavy load and is ready for the body to be installed, probably a medium dump unit.

quarter-doors on all standard cab versions. Standard bed sizes were 5.5 feet, 6.5 feet, and 8 feet, with Flareside models restricted to just the 6.5-foot bed. Two Triton V-8 engines were offered: the 4.6-liter or 5.4-liter. Four-wheel anti-lock disc brakes were now standard on all F-150s. To maintain sales volume, the company kept the prior generation F-150 in production as the new models were introduced and production ramped up.

2005–2008

In the 2004 model year the all-new F-150 hadn't offered a six-cylinder engine, but for 2005 the reliable and economical 4.2-liter 202-horsepower Triton six was offered, along with a 5-speed manual transmission. The company also rolled out all-new Super Duty pickups this year.

Ford introduced the new Freestyle as its crossover SUV for 2005. Larger than the Escape, the Freestyle was more car-like than the Explorer, and it featured a continuously variable transmission (CVT) for better fuel economy.

To help maintain its title as best-selling vehicle in America, the F-150s received new styling updates for 2006, with new front bumpers, grilles, and headlamps. In 2007 a flexible-fuel version of the Triton 5.4-liter was added. This new version could run on E85, which is a mixture of 85 percent ethanol and 15 percent gasoline. Popular in the Corn Belt, which supplies much of the corn used to make ethanol fuel, the E85 trucks never caught on with the general population. More exciting news was the new supercharged Ford F-150 Harley-Davidson. In addition, a new F-450 medium job was added to the Super Duty lineup with a 3-ton payload rating and the ability to tow more than 24,000 pounds. Also in 2007 was a new FX2 Sport package for XLT SuperCab and SuperCrew trucks.

The Explorer got a freshening up for 2006 with more aggressive styling, a new interior, and a revised and improved chassis that included a more potent V-8.

Ford introduced another new crossover SUV for 2007—the Edge. With crisp, European styling and a smooth, refined passenger-car chassis, the midsized sport utility vehicle offered four trim versions in all.

Another anniversary was reached in 2008: the sixtieth anniversary of the F-series trucks. To celebrate, Ford offered Special Edition commemorative models with significant improvements: a new tailgate-mounted rear-vision camera, a remote-start system, and an increase in maximum towing capacity to 11,000 pounds.

You have to love this picture! It shows a 2008 F-150 four-door pickup towing a trailer that holds a vintage 1948 Ford F-1 pickup. The sixty-year age difference is very revealing in that it shows how much larger—and plusher—trucks have grown over the years.

THE ROAD BACK

The top-selling Ford F-150, America's perennial favorite vehicle, received some important updates for 2009, namely a lighter but stronger frame, a Roll Stability Control system, improvements to the front and rear suspensions, and a new Trailer Sway Control system. Two-door cabs were once again available. Styling was more aggressive than before, with looks similar to the big Super Duty models. The new Ford trucks were quieter, smoother-riding, and better-built. Company engineers worked hard to eliminate many small irritations, such as the steering wheel's tendency to vibrate at idle, common on previous models. Other improvements included the addition of a 6-speed transmission, front side-impact and side-curtain air bags, and a larger crew cab with a flat rear floor. A new premium F-150 Platinum model was targeted at luxury truck buyers.

The Raptor was a new model for 2010, developed by the Ford skunk works design team known as the Special Vehicle Team, or SVT. In this image you can see the side steps and special wheels that came with this impressive machine.

Ford introduced a new seven-passenger SUV for 2009, the Flex. A large wagon-type vehicle, it was unique in being based on a lightweight crossover chassis. Powered by a V-6 engine, it offered scads of room along with good fuel economy and great styling.

But there were big problems with the US auto industry, and they became very apparent this year. The Big Three's share of the total automotive market had been declining for years, and in the passenger car segment the decrease had been almost catastrophic. Market share had eroded along with profit margins, and the US makers were losing money. American automakers were also saddled with staggering legacy costs that included paying thousands of laid-off workers and retired workers, plus exorbitant health care costs along with regular cost-of-living increases, all this a result of contracts agreed to in better times. The US companies were straining under a crushing load of debt and obligations that by now had become unsustainable. For years truck profits had been propping up the Big Three, but when dramatically higher gasoline prices and a worsening economy began to sharply reduce demand in the truck segment, the companies found themselves in serious trouble. Shockingly, both GM and Chrysler were forced to declare bankruptcy and seek government bailouts. Ford management, however, had seen the crisis coming early enough and mortgaged many of its assets prior to its arrival in order to build a substantial

An extended cab F-150, this one a 2009 model, looks sharp with its black grille and window trim, and spoked alloy wheels. This was an extremely difficult year for the domestic automobile industry as Ford rivals General Motors and Chrysler struggled to avoid bankruptcy.

Chapter 9

America's favorite vehicle, the Ford F-150, returned for 2009 with several improvements, including a lighter, stronger frame and revised front and rear suspensions for improved ride, handling, and stability.

war chest—or cash cushion, take your pick—and thus was spared the embarrassment of having to go hat in hand to the government to beg a loan. Instead, the company got to work developing new models to stimulate demand and to reorganize the company for better efficiency. The program, called "One Ford," would yield important economies that would enable Ford to weather the economic storm and continue its leadership position in the truck market.

One of the most painful steps was to convert some of its truck plants over to building small, economical cars, which suddenly were in demand. The problem was that small cars generated small profits, nothing compared to the big margins earned on trucks. But with truck demand so low the company had excess plant capacity dedicated to vehicles that were slow sellers.

2010–2012

For the next several years the US automakers focused on recovering from the sharp economic downturn of 2009. One thing Ford management emphasized from 2010 to 2012 was its plan to utilize its worldwide development resources and product range

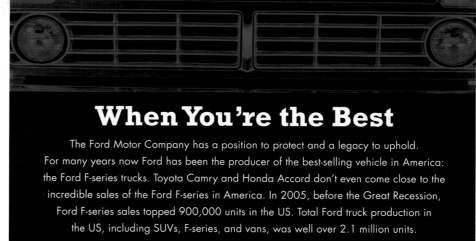

When You're the Best

The Ford Motor Company has a position to protect and a legacy to uphold. For many years now Ford has been the producer of the best-selling vehicle in America: the Ford F-series trucks. Toyota Camry and Honda Accord don't even come close to the incredible sales of the Ford F-series in America. In 2005, before the Great Recession, Ford F-series sales topped 900,000 units in the US. Total Ford truck production in the US, including SUVs, F-series, and vans, was well over 2.1 million units.

to field new products quicker and at lower cost. A prime example was the new Transit Connect work van introduced for 2010. With a lightweight chassis, roomy and boxy body shape, and an economical four-cylinder engine, the European-style Transit Connect was a popular product in overseas markets, and now Ford brought it to America. Built in Turkey, it offered steel sides or optional side and rear windows.

There was a hot new F-150 Raptor model for 2010, a product of Ford's now-legendary Special Vehicle Team (formerly Special Vehicle Operations). The Raptor offered a new heavy-duty suspension along with a 400-horsepower 6.2-liter V-8 engine. Expensive and highly desirable, it was a halo truck that was also a solid profit-earner.

For 2011 the Explorer line was restyled on a new unibody platform. The unibody design endowed the Explorer with a lower weight, better handling, a refined ride, and important fuel economy improvements. The Explorer now rode more like a car than a truck, important in this market segment, and boasted a smooth 3.5-liter V-6 teamed to a 6-speed automatic transmission. It was important to focus as much attention on trucks now because things had turned completely around, and now the passenger car market was practically in free fall while truck demand was surging.

The 2011 F-150 trucks were offered in XL, STX, XLT, King Ranch, Lariat, Platinum, and off-road FX4 versions. The F-150 line got all-new engines for 2011, including two new V-8s, a new base six, and an optional hot new EcoBoost 3.5-liter V-6. It provided the power of a 365-horsepower V-8 with the fuel economy of a six.

The Super Duty line received new exterior styling upgrades that included a new front fascia. Its engines were upgraded to better compete with the powerful new GM and Dodge heavy-duty trucks. At the 2011 Chicago Auto Show, Ford claimed that the new models had the thickest-gauge steel frame of any heavy-duty truck. The 2011 Ford F-Series Super Duty was awarded *Truckin* magazine's "Topline Power Puller" award for 2011. It also won *Popular Mechanics* magazine's "Best Workhorse" award.

Doesn't this look like fun! A 2011 Ford Escape out looking for adventure in Alaska. This year the Escape continued as one of the top-selling SUVs in America.

For the 2012 model year, the midsized crossover Ford Edge was given a major freshening with styling revisions, a new interior, and a new 3.5-liter V-6 that produced a surprisingly robust 265 horsepower. Also available on the Edge was a 240-horsepower EcoBoost four-cylinder engine that provided the power of a six with the fuel economy of a four. This year the F-150 Harley-Davidson model was also the beneficiary of a freshening. The F-250 Super Duty trucks now offered a 400-horsepower turbodiesel engine.

2013–2017

At the 2013 North American International Auto Show (NAIAS)—more commonly called the Detroit Auto Show—Ford unveiled an exciting new Transit commercial van. Developed under the "One Ford" global development program, the new Transit was co-engineered and designed by Ford of Europe and Ford engineers in North America. It offered several distinct body versions, including high-roof models, and was planned to replace the Econoline van. The Econoline, however, remains in the Ford lineup at this writing in cutaway chassis-cab models.

The 2013 Escape was all new and designed in conjunction with the European Ford Kuga, and it was better-handling and more economical than before. Sales volume, already excellent, began to climb toward the 300,000 annual mark.

A new Ford Explorer Sport was announced in early 2012 as a 2013 model. The Sport trim included black exterior treatments, stiffer chassis and suspension, larger brakes, and an EcoBoost 3.5-liter twin-turbo V-6 pumping out 365 horsepower.

Because of its new chassis design, the all-new 2011 Explorer rode more like a car than a truck, which was an important advantage in this market segment. The Explorer also boasted a smooth 3.5-liter V-6 teamed to a 6-speed automatic transmission.

Here's a pretty sharp-looking F-150—we especially like those wheels! The US economy, which hit a low point in 2009, was beginning to come back. Trucks such as this one were one reason why shoppers were returning to showrooms.

F-150s received mostly minor changes for 2014. The Escape, being all new for 2013, was likewise essentially carryover for 2014. By now the US economy was once again on the upswing and trucks were selling well.

There weren't many changes to the 2015 F-150 either. Ford had an all-new truck coming out the following year and was focusing its attention on that one.

In fact, the entirely new F-150 designed for the 2016 model year was revolutionary. Without making the truck smaller—indeed without significantly changing any dimensions—Ford engineers were able to cut the weight of these pickups by some 750 pounds by making the bodies out of aluminum alloy. Because of the weight reduction, even the base 3.5-liter V-6 engine fitted as standard equipment could haul a decent load. The combination of a smaller engine and lower weight also yielded important fuel economy gains for Ford buyers. The F-150 was now rated at 18 miles per gallon in the city and up to 25 miles per gallon on the highway, mileage figures that once would have been considered excellent for a subcompact car. Best of all, the Fords lost nothing in capability but showed noticeable improvements in ride and handling. Assembly of the new body required an expensive tear-up and reworking of the assembly line. After that it took a while before production ramped up to prior levels, but in time it did. By 2016 Ford's truck lines were humming smoothly with all models available.

In September 2015 Ford unveiled the 2017 Ford Super Duty line at the State Fair of Texas, because Texas is a crucial truck market. It marked the first all-new Super Duty line since the line's 1998 debut. The body, like the F-150s, is made of military-grade aluminum alloy. Thus, for the first time since 1996, the Super Duty and F-150 lines share essentially the same cab. In switching to an aluminum body, the 2017 Super Duty now weighs up to 350 pounds less than comparable 2016 models. To create an even stronger truck than before, Ford engineers strengthened the frame and drivetrain with fortified driveshafts, axles, and brakes. The F-250 and F-350 pickups utilize a fully boxed frame; chassis-cab models are produced on a frame boxed up to the rear of the cab and of c-channel design from there on back. The 2017 Super Duty power choices include a 6.2-liter gasoline V-8, a 6.8-liter V-10 (F-450 and up), or a 6.7-liter diesel V-8. The F-250 features a TorqShift 6-speed automatic while all other Super Duty trucks are paired with the 6R140 6-speed automatic. Super Duty trim levels include XL, XLT, Lariat, King Ranch, and Platinum. Cab configurations are two-door standard cab, four-door SuperCab, and four-door SuperCrew. The trucks are available in F-250, F-350, and F-450 pickup truck models as well as F-350, F-450, and F-550 chassis-cab models. Base prices in the United States range from $32,535 (F-250 XL) to $77,125 (F-450 Platinum).

Ford proudly calls the 2017 Super Duty lineup "The Best-Selling Heavy-Duty Pickup Truck" in America. The heavy-duty "work pickup" line consists of F-250, F-350, F-450, and F-550 Super Duty, and the medium-duty F-650 and F-750. Rugged, dependable trucks that are among the most coveted work vehicles in the world.

The F-series remains the best-selling vehicle in America. In addition, Ford's truck line includes the top-selling Escape, the Edge, the still-popular Explorer, and the Expedition, plus passenger and commercial versions of the Transit and Transit Connect.

But 2017 is especially important in Ford history, because it marks one hundred years of producing genuine American trucks, a feat that is even more impressive when one thinks about the millions upon millions of trucks the company has built and the millions of them that are in service every day across America and the world. Ford's contribution to trucking is monumental, and the company's contribution to America is priceless.

Here's the Ford Expedition for 2017, part of the hottest-selling line of trucks in America. Note the massive alloy wheels and abundance of bright trim.

Shown here is a really nicely spec'd truck. It's a 2017 F-150 SuperCab with the Special Edition package, which adds lots of blackout trim, a black grille, special wheels, and bold "hockey stick" side stripes.

INDEX

ABOUT THE AUTHOR

One of America's best-known automotive journalists is Patrick Foster, a dedicated historian and author who has been writing for more than twenty-five years. Foster is a feature writer and also has regular columns in *Hemmings Classic Car* and *Old Cars Weekly*. He has written twenty-two books and contributed material to several others.

Foster has won numerous writing awards, including the AACA's prestigious Thomas McKean Memorial Cup for the best book of automotive history for 1998. In 1997 one of his works was named Outstanding Periodical Article by the Society of Automotive Historians. In 2011 Foster was honored with the Lee Iacocca Award, perhaps the most coveted award in the car hobby, for excellence in automotive writing. The 2015 International Automotive Media Competition (IAMC) saw him bring home a silver medal for an article on the 1930–1934 Nash automobiles, and a bronze medal for his book *Jeep: The History of America's Greatest Vehicle*. In 2016 Foster again took home two awards from the IAMC event when *International Harvester Trucks: The Complete History* won a silver medal and an article on George Romney was awarded a bronze. Foster's books can be purchased at his personal website www.oldemilfordpress.com.